Advance Praise for Yoga for Paddling

"Anna has sold me on *Yoga for Paddling* for sure. I need to balance my body to keep paddling into my sixties, and *Yoga for Paddling* provides clear and well-written information to help me accomplish that."
—*Sean Morley, accomplished coach, expedition, and surf kayaker who completed the first solo circumnavigation of the UK and Ireland by sea kayak*

"Anna has been a huge mentor for me and pushes every human to be the best human they can be. *Yoga for Paddling* is a great addition to paddlers' libraries for helping to reduce the aches and pains of everyday life and kayaking. Keep this book close by both on your paddling trips and at home."
—*Adriene Levknecht,* Canoe & Kayak *magazine's 2016 Female Paddler of the Year and eight-time Green River Race Champion*

"*Yoga for Paddling* has inspired me to bring more balance to my body by making time for yoga practice in my fitness routine. Anna's book provides helpful information and guidance to help me get started and develop an effective practice."
—*Travis Grant, two-time Molokai to Oahu SUP Champion, Battle of the Paddle SUP long distance champion*

"As an avid canoeist for over thirty years, I sometimes worry about how my body will handle the next thirty. With *Yoga for Paddling* as a guide, I am confident that I can balance and maintain the strength and flexibility I need to continue in the sport I love. Thanks to Anna's well-laid-out book, I look forward to canoeing with my grandchildren someday."
—*Eli Helbert, five-time Open Canoe Freestyle Rodeo World Champion, eleven-time North American Open Canoe Slalom Champion, and first Open Canoe to race the Green River Narrows*

Paul Villecourt

Heidi,
It was wonderful to
have you in the
training this week!
I look forward to
paddling with you
again soon!

xo
Anna

Yoga for Paddling

KAYAKERS, CANOEISTS, AND STAND-UP PADDLERS

Anna Levesque
Photographs by Scott Martin

GUILFORD, CONNECTICUT

FALCON®

An imprint of Globe Pequot
Falcon and FalconGuides are registered trademarks and Make Adventure Your Story is a trademark of Rowman & Littlefield.

Distributed by NATIONAL BOOK NETWORK

British Library Cataloguing-in-Publication Information available

Library of Congress Cataloging-in-Publication Data

Names: Levesque, Anna, author.
Title: Yoga for paddling : kayakers, canoeists, and stand-up paddlers / Anna Levesque ;
  photographs by Scott Martin.
Description: Guilford, Connecticut : FALCON, [2017] | Includes bibliographical references
  and index.
Identifiers: LCCN 2016047033 (print) | LCCN 2016051793 (ebook) | ISBN 9781493028689 (pbk.)
  | ISBN 9781493028696 (e-book)
Subjects: LCSH: Hatha yoga. | Outdoor life—Health aspects.
Classification: LCC RA781.7 .L477 2017 (print) | LCC RA781.7 (ebook) | DDC
  613.7/046—dc23
LC record available at https://lccn.loc.gov/2016047033

∞™ The paper used in this publication meets the minimum requirements of American National Standard for Information Sciences—Permanence of Paper for Printed Library Materials, ANSI/ NISO Z39.48-1992.

Printed in the United States of America

CONTENTS

ACKNOWLEDGMENTS

I'd like to acknowledge my yoga and Ayurveda teachers, and their teachers, and their teachers, and so on, going back many generations. I have a lot of gratitude for Joe Taft and Deirdre Smith-Gilmer for being thoughtful, effective, and inspiring alignment-based yoga teachers. They've had a big impact on my practice and on my teaching. I'd like to acknowledge Vishnu Das and Indu Arora for teaching me about the subtle aspects of yoga and helping me to dive deeper into Ayurveda, the science of life. Thank you, Dave Costello, for advocating for this book and to Katie Benoit and Meredith Dias for being great editors to work with. I'm grateful for Libby Hinsley, a caring and effective yoga teacher, yoga therapist, and physical therapist whose input and time were key in this book coming together. I acknowledge Scott Martin for his dedication to his work and for photographing the lovely images contained in this book. I'm thankful for the loving, supportive relationships in my life, both in the paddling community and in the yoga and Ayurvedic communities. Thanks to Justin at Tidal Trails for generously driving us around by boat for the photo shoot in South Carolina. Special gratitude goes to my loving, compassionate husband, Andrew Holcombe, who unwaveringly supports me on my journey of self-knowledge. I want to also thank you, the reader, for delving into this book. May it be of service to your mind, to your body, and to your paddling. May it help you paddle with ease, comfort, skill, strength, and balance for many, many years to come. Namaste.

Paul Villecourt

FOREWORD

IF YOU ARE A PADDLER OF ANY SORT, this book is for you. As a physical therapist and longtime yoga practitioner and instructor, I'm so happy to see this book come to fruition. I've had the privilege of getting to know Anna Levesque in several different contexts over the past few years, and there is no one more perfectly suited to bring you the valuable information you'll find in the following pages.

I have witnessed what I can only describe as Anna's devotion to water and all its qualities—the power and persistence of it, the awe-inspiring thrill of it, and its ability to constantly adapt and change according to its circumstance. Embracing the qualities of the water element can help us learn to go with the flow of life and find greater ease amid the reality of change. Anna is a great example of this, as she embodies many of these qualities in her work as a paddler, an instructor, and a yogini.

Anna educates and inspires people all over the world to embrace their own power and the power of water through paddlesports. As a yoga instructor, her thoughtfulness and high level of integrity are refreshing. As a yoga practitioner, I've seen her take to heart many of the valuable lessons she presents to you in this book. Through thoughtful and subtle work in her practice, she has truly found a way to maintain structural balance for herself and bring herself out of the pain of injury.

I began my own exploration of healing through yoga when, in my early twenties, I found myself in near-daily pain in my low back, hips, knees, and feet. For me, my struggles were largely the result of hypermobility and the effect of many years of competitive sports that left my body out of balance.

It would take me many years of yoga study and practice to fully understand many of the important messages that Anna presents in this yoga book—that it isn't about getting a posture "right" or going farther into a pose. Yoga is an invitation inward, and the practice of postures is an opportunity to understand your body more fully, and to understand what your body needs to regain balance and stability. As I now approach my fortieth birthday, I am happy to say my body is happier than it has been at any point in my adult life.

I started teaching yoga in 2005 and quickly discovered a desire to learn more about the body and its capacity for structural balance and healing. This led me to pursue physical therapy training. Since 2011 I have practiced physical therapy primarily in an outpatient orthopedic setting and integrated yoga into my practice to help others. It has been deeply rewarding.

I recently had the pleasure of treating Anna in my private physical therapy practice, Yoga Rx of Asheville. She came to me with hip pain and shoulder pain, both of which could be traced back to the chronic muscular imbalance brought about by many years of paddling. Through our work together, I learned a lot about how paddlers use their bodies, and how taxing those movements can be for certain areas of the body. We worked with manual techniques to release some chronic myofascial tension patterns, and we tailored her home yoga practice to help bring balance back to her body. The result has been wildly successful!

When I recently got into one of Anna's kayaks to feel the positioning and movements of kayaking, I was shocked at how fatigued my hip flexors and upper trapezius felt after just a few minutes of bracing myself in the kayak while performing the motion of paddling. I knew then just how important this book would be to those who spend many hours on a regular basis doing these movements.

I hope you will use this book as a guide to develop your own home yoga practice so that you are able to enjoy many more years on the water with greater ease and comfort in body and mind. Yoga encourages individuals to cultivate a calm mind in the presence of life's constantly fluctuating extremes. I imagine adventures on water bring about a similar inward focus. Aside from the thrill, power, and awe that paddling sports bring to your life, I hope that you will also savor the peace, stillness, persistence, and adaptability that water represents, and that you find these qualities reflected in yourself through your yoga practice.

Libby Hinsley, PT, C-IAYT, E-RYT 500
Licensed Physical Therapist, Certified Yoga Therapist,
and Yoga Teacher Trainer
Asheville Holistic Physical Therapy
Asheville, North Carolina

INTRODUCTION

MY LOVE OF YOGA STARTED IN THE MID-1990S in the living room of a fellow raft guide in West Virginia. We would gather around her TV and practice with yoga videos on VHS. Moving my body through the yoga sequences felt just as fluid, challenging, and satisfying as maneuvering my kayak through the currents on the river. Both challenged me, and brought balance, energy, and contentment to my life.

I remember writing the list of poses from the videos down on sheets of notepaper so that I could practice anywhere. I carried them with me to the sandy beaches of remote rivers in the Ecuadorian Amazon, to small riverside villages suspended in time in Mexico, and to pristine whitewater accessed

Practicing open rooftop yoga in Mexico.

Anna on the podium at the 2001 World Freestyle Championships in Sort, Spain.

only by helicopter in New Zealand. When I started competing on the international whitewater kayak freestyle circuit, I found that my yoga practice brought steadiness to my nomadic lifestyle. It helped me deal with the stress, self-doubt, and anxiety that I experienced competing and running extreme whitewater. I attribute my success in reaching the podium at the 2001 World Freestyle Championships, and my success in competition in general, to my daily yoga practice.

I've spent over twenty years paddling an average of 200-plus days per year. I've healed the few instances of chronic pain I've experienced, and I haven't suffered any major injuries. Imbalances, misalignments, and muscle tweaks have come up, and the self-awareness that yoga has helped me develop has allowed me to recognize and address them quickly and effectively. I believe that the physical, mental, and emotional benefits of yoga have helped me to successfully face challenges on and off the water. From bringing alignment to my body, to helping me face grief with compassion and grace, yoga has helped to keep me healthy, strong,

Frankenstein rapid on the
Narrows of Green River,
North Carolina.

and supple in mind and body. It is one of the reasons I feel like I am in the best shape ever, and more content in my forties than at any other time in my life.

A vigorous yoga practice is what attracted me in my twenties. I viewed yoga poses as something to strive for, and getting a workout as an important aspect of yoga. In my drive to get "good" at vigorous flow yoga, I moved through poses quickly without attention to alignment, exacerbating imbalances in my body and increasing my risk for injury. I was introduced to alignment-based yoga in my thirties, during my 200-hour yoga teacher training, and a whole new world of self-awareness opened up. I was learning what my body actually needed, versus what my ego wanted me to practice to look good.

As my practice deepened and I pursued my 500-hour yoga teacher training certification, I delved deeper into the more subtle benefits of yoga. The ancient concept that the ultimate

" I WAS LEARNING WHAT MY BODY ACTUALLY NEEDED, VERSUS WHAT MY EGO WANTED ME TO PRACTICE TO LOOK GOOD.

expression of a pose requires both steadiness and ease became the focus of my practice. I learned how to bring both to my practice with subtle alignment cues from experienced and effective teachers. I was amazed at the strength I was cultivating by learning to move more slowly. I was able to become aware of and activate muscles that had been getting sleepy due to kayaking and address imbalances exacerbated due to a vigorous practice that was, at times, driven by ego.

Over the last two decades, both my paddling and my yoga practice have shifted and changed. I still have a passion for paddling, challenging myself and improving. But my passions now focus on learning to paddle surf and challenging myself on my stand-up paddleboard (SUP) rather than ticking off difficult rivers or learning the latest freestyle tricks in my whitewater kayak. I'm also a passionate instructor, guide, and instructor trainer who finds great joy in empowering and inspiring paddlers

Paddlesurfing in Waikiki, Hawaii.

Reid Inouye

both on and off the water. I've dedicated the last twelve years to my company, Girls at Play, which supports women in building skill and increasing confidence through whitewater kayaking, yoga, SUP, and travel.

My yoga practice has become a tool that supports my body's ability to practice and teach the paddlesports that I love with comfort, ease, and skill. It also supports the more subtle practices of breathwork and meditation that help me manage stress, cultivate mental clarity, and keep my energy levels steady. I think that one of the best reasons to practice yoga for paddling is the self-care to be able to paddle well into your eighties!

Last fall I started feeling some pain and discomfort in my left shoulder girdle. I had been paddling a lot and not giving my yoga practice as much attention. At the put-in to a Class IV river, I raised my arms to pull my drysuit gasket over my head and my left shoulder gave out. It wasn't dislocated or sublexed; it was a tweak in my shoulder muscles that was debilitating. Instead of running the river, I drove shuttle and waited at the take-out, working my shoulder out with a tennis ball and some yoga poses.

Within a few days I was in my PT/yoga therapist's office. We worked together on exercises, movements, and poses that would help heal the injury. Within two weeks I was pain free, feeling strong, and back on the water. Having the tools, knowledge, and resources to heal and prevent injuries is key for paddling performance and longevity. Yoga is a resource that has been exceptionally helpful for me as a paddler, and my intention with this book is to share the knowledge I've gained so that it may in turn be of benefit to you.

I've seen the catchphrase "health is wealth" show up a lot lately in the media and on social media. I think it's an important concept to spread. There is more to health than getting outside and exercising. Yes, paddling and staying fit are pieces of overall health, but there are other pieces including diet, lifestyle, self-care, and relaxation.

During my 500-hour teacher training program, I was also introduced to Ayurveda, the 5,000-year-old sister science to yoga based on diet and lifestyle that translates as "science of life." It is an ancient system of health based on

> **THERE IS MORE TO HEALTH THAN GETTING OUTSIDE AND EXERCISING . . . INCLUDING DIET, LIFESTYLE, SELF-CARE, AND RELAXATION.**

the elements and qualities of nature with a focus on cultivating well-being and longevity through self-knowledge. After a few months of making changes in my diet and lifestyle using Ayurveda, my digestion improved, I shed weight, and my energy levels soared. I was so impressed by the results that I decided to enroll in a yearlong Ayurveda Health Counselor program, which I graduated from in 2016. This has added another element to my ability to coach and assist paddlers in cultivating vitality and longevity on and off the water.

I'm an advocate of self-study and self-knowledge. I don't expect your experience to be like my experience, and I don't expect you to practice yoga just like I do. Having said that, there are some movements in paddling that generally lead to the same imbalances in every paddler's body, and that's what I'm focusing on in this book. My intention is to share the knowledge that I've gained over the last twenty years of combining yoga with paddling so that others may benefit from my experience. I've consulted with my physical therapist/yoga therapist to ensure that the anatomy and alignment presented in this book are accurate, effective, and practical. I've invited paddlers from different disciplines to contribute comments, suggestions, and experiences. I hope this book will contribute to your health, vitality, alignment, and longevity on and off the water.

The first chapter gives a basic overview of yoga followed by an exploration of some proven benefits of yoga. The following two chapters focus on the anatomy of paddling and the alignment principles that are most important for helping bring paddlers' bodies back into optimal alignment. These chapters are meant to be a resource that sets the reader up to better understand the body mechanics of paddling and the impact that paddling has on the body. These are also chapters that the reader can refer back to while practicing the poses in later chapters, or to clarify anatomy or alignment questions that come up.

Chapter 4 focuses on the importance of optimal breathing for yoga and for navigating the stressors of daily life both on and off the water. Chapter 5 introduces yoga props that you can use in your practice to assist your body in moving toward optimal alignment. Chapters 6 through 11 guide you step-by-step through yoga poses that help the body activate muscles that are underactive while paddling, and cultivate suppleness in the muscles that are overactive in paddling. Cues for the alignment principles are included in the description of each pose. These chapters are organized by muscle groups so that the reader can easily access poses that target a particular set of muscles. Chapter 12 outlines the

Anna Levesque

benefits of relaxation for health and performance. Chapter 13 provides guidance on how to sequence the yoga poses in this book to create routines for your home practice, and chapter 14 introduces the basics of SUP yoga.

This book is not meant to be the complete work on every aspect of anatomy or yoga for paddling. Yoga is thousands of years old and has several different lineages and styles, and there are hundreds of yoga poses. It would be impossible for this, or any book, to cover it all. It is also impossible to cover every possible muscle imbalance in every paddling body. One of the purposes of this book is to provide effective information that will help paddlers balance some of the most common imbalances caused by paddling.

WHAT IS YOGA?

THE WORD *YOGA* MEANS "TO YOKE" OR "UNION." We can also think of it as connection. It is an ancient system of self-study that allows practitioners to connect with their true selves beyond the thought patterns and fluctuations of the mind. Through the practice of physical postures (asana), yoga helps us cultivate awareness of the present moment. Ever notice that your thoughts are most commonly about the future or the past? The past is already done; we can learn from it, but there is nothing that we can do to change it. The future hasn't happened yet, and there are millions of possibilities for what can happen. Life happens now, and yet we are often too caught up in the past or in the future to be present in the now. Yoga helps us to become present to who we really are, and how we are living our lives moment to moment.

Paddling also brings us to present moment awareness. Whether you're paddling into a challenging rapid, on an open ocean swell, or through the quiet morning mist of a glassy lake, thoughts, worries, and stress fade away. What's left is a feeling of connectedness with that moment and the beauty of nature, exhilaration, peacefulness—whatever you are experiencing at that moment. I would also call that yoga practice.

In addition to connection to our authentic selves, to the present moment, to our bodies and to nature, yoga also helps us remember our connection to each other. The practice of yoga challenges us to step outside of our egos and cultivate compassion for ourselves and for others, remembering that we are more alike than we are different. My favorite yoga/water metaphor comes from master yoga teacher Erich Schiffman, who writes, "Ego is when the wave—you or me—mistakenly believes

Opposite: Capturing the light at Kiawah Island, South Carolina.

Paddling at dusk on Lake Jocassee, South Carolina.

that it stands alone and that, somehow, it is essentially separate and different from the ocean and from other waves. . . . We are both the wave, individual and unique, *and* the ocean. Both. At the same time."[1]

What most people in the United States have come to refer to as yoga are the physical postures (asana) that we practice in yoga classes. This is not completely accurate, as the system of yoga has eight limbs, physical postures being only one of the eight, with breathwork (pranayama) and meditation (dhyana) being two others. The original purpose of yoga postures was to prepare the body to sit comfortably in meditation for long periods of time. There are many lineages of yoga, and part of the journey is to find the lineage or style that works best for you and your body. It is an individual journey that leads to greater self-awareness.

Opposite: Striking a pose at Elves Chasm in Grand Canyon.

I like to compare the yogic system to a trip I took down the Grand Canyon. As a whitewater paddle, the big-water rapids were what first got me interested in the trip. Once I was in the canyon, I realized that the paddling was only a piece of the experience that is a Grand Canyon river trip. The side hikes, the beauty, the history, the geology, the sacredness, the river tribe, the stars at night, camp life, being on the river for sixteen days, and the paddling all make up the awesomeness of the trip. There's nothing wrong with paddling the Grand Canyon just for the rapids, and there's nothing wrong with practicing yoga just for the physical benefits. Having said that, I'd like to offer every reader the possibility to delve deeper into the practice of the eight limbs of yoga if it calls to you.

The Benefits of Yoga

The practice of yoga postures was traditionally taught one-on-one, with the teacher designing a unique sequence that benefitted the specific health concerns and problems of the student. Now there are over 36 million yoga practitioners in the United States, according to the 2016 Yoga in America study conducted by *Yoga Journal* and the Yoga Alliance Foundation. This means that yoga is now most often taught in a group setting. There are hundreds of studies touting the positive benefits of yoga on health and wellness, including stress reduction, relaxation, strength, flexibility, better alignment, balance, better sleep, focus, mental clarity, and more.

The Yoga in America study found that 75 percent of yoga practitioners self-report being physically strong compared to 57 percent of non-practitioners, and 86 percent of yoga practitioners report having a strong sense of mental clarity, compared to 77 percent of non-practitioners.

The National Center for Complementary and Integrative Health conducted a study of ninety people with chronic low-back pain and found that participants who practiced an alignment-based style of yoga for six months experienced significantly less disability, pain, and depression.

> " [PEOPLE] WHO PRACTICED AN ALIGNMENT-BASED STYLE OF YOGA FOR SIX MONTHS EXPERIENCED SIGNIFICANTLY LESS DISABILITY, PAIN, AND DEPRESSION.

A study by John Derringer, a psychiatrist at Harvard Medical School, found that people who use "mind-body medicine

Wild Thing on the beach in Kiawah Island, South Carolina.

interventions" that include yoga and meditation are 43 percent less likely to visit the hospital, be ordered a medical test by their doctor, or need emergency care, compared to those who did not use such practices.[2]

Derringer has also studied the effects of mind-body therapies such as yoga and meditation on genes that govern immune function and stress. He found that the practices have the effect of switching some related genes on and off. "There is a true biological effect," he told *Bloomberg News* in an interview. "The kinds of things that happen when you meditate do have effects throughout the body, not just in the brain."[3]

Yoga is also catching on as an important cross training activity for professional and Olympic athletes. In a 2014 interview with *Sports Illustrated* reporter Peter King, Aaron Rodgers, quarterback for the Green Bay Packers, talked about the benefits he experienced during the 2014 off-season:

In the first three months of the off-season, I did a ton of yoga. I hadn't done that much of that before. I loved it. Absolutely loved it. The stretching, the atmosphere, the group setting, a teacher helping you get the maximum flexibility . . . I felt so great after those sessions. My sleep improved . . . My energy improved . . . I feel a lot better right now.

According to his NFL stats, it turned out to be his second-best season so far.[4]

In another *Sports Illustrated* article published in 2014, top athletes including Lebron James, Kareem Abdul-Jabbar, Kevin Love, Dwyane Wade, Kevin Durant, and Kevin Garnett touted the benefits of yoga for basketball. In that same article, Gwen Lawrence, a yoga instructor for the New York Giants, is quoted as saying: "It's more than just flexibility work—yoga also helps balance the body. Because if there's an imbalance in the body and [players are] working out really hard and training and lifting and running, they're just going to be training that imbalance. So it's really important I help them get balanced."[5]

To me whitewater kayaking mirrors life off the water. When I'm paddling a rapid, it's important that I look where I want to go and not at the obstacles that are in my way. If I stare at a big rock in the middle of a rapid, I end up hitting it. If I keep my eyes on the current that takes me away or past the rock, then I end up missing the rock. This reminds me that when I set goals it's important to focus on the goal and not let myself get distracted by the challenges that arise.

Lawrence's comment speaks directly to the intention of this book, which is to balance the imbalances caused by the motions of paddling, whether that be paddling a kayak, a canoe, or a SUP. An example of how yoga can contribute to the healing of paddling injuries is the story of Andrew Holcombe, two-time Green Race champion, silver medalist at the 2003 World Kayak Freestyle Championships, and three-time US National Kayak Freestyle Team member.

In 2010, at the age of twenty-nine, Andrew was experiencing so much pain in his low back and right hip that he could barely stand up once he got out of bed. He had been feeling discomfort in these areas, but because he was young and healthy he thought it would resolve itself. He describes himself at that time as being "stubborn" and "in denial that something was actually wrong." Eventually the pain got so bad that he could no longer ignore it. He went to see his doctor, who delivered the diagnosis of disk herniations in L4 and L5.

"My PT told me there were two paths to resolving the problem, one that involved surgery, and one that involved alternative work including chiropractic, yoga, and physical therapy. After consultations and research I came to understand that if I could manage my pain in the short-term, the non-surgical option offered the opportunity of fully healing. Surgery had the potential for future complications due to the fusing of my disks. I didn't want to fuse my spine if I didn't have to. To me it was worth trying out the alternative practices for eight months to see if they worked before jumping into surgery."

Andrew approached his healing like he approaches training for a kayak competition—all in and looking to win. His discipline was extraordinary. He took eight months off from kayaking, which was no small feat for someone who is a third-generation paddler on both sides of the family and first went down a river in a raft at the age of six months with his mom (a raft guide on the Nantahala River). In addition to giving up his passion for several months, he also had to forgo the opportunity to defend his Green River Race title that year. I witnessed and supported this healing journey firsthand, because, in addition to being an accomplished whitewater paddler, Andrew is also my husband. For close to a year he dedicated himself to physical therapy, yoga, and chiropractic. He practiced every day, and the only other exercise he did was walking and hiking.

> I love how water ebbs and flows, reminding me that there are natural rhythms to nature and to life. Life is more effortless when I accept whatever phase I find myself in. Water does not only flow in one direction.

"All I could do was walk, physical therapy, and yoga. Yoga provided active healing that worked not only to restore the parts of my body that were broken, but also to keep the rest of my body working and healthy during the healing process."

After eight months Andrew's disks healed, the pain was gone, and he was able to start kayaking again. He competed in the Green Race a few months after the healing process was complete and placed fifth. He has since been pain free and is back competing and paddling at a high level. He continues to integrate yoga into his life as a way to prevent future and recurring injuries.

"Yoga keeps my muscles bendy, and what alignment yoga really does for me is work all the little stabilizing muscles that keep everything in place and keep everything working. I prefer relaxing, calming yoga that focuses on alignment because everything else in my life is so active and strength building. There's a branch of yoga for everyone, and that's what I like."

Andrew is not alone in his experience. I've heard other paddlers tell similar stories of recovering from injury with the help of yoga. Instead of waiting until there is serious injury, I wanted to encourage paddlers to work toward alignment and balance using yoga as a preventive measure. Andrew's disk herniations didn't happen in one incident, it was the cumulative strain on his back from carrying his kayak, sitting in his kayak, and paddling long hours day after day without any counterbalancing activity. In fact, instead of counterbalancing activities, he would often go mountain biking as cross training. There's nothing wrong with mountain biking, but when you look at the body positioning, it is very similar to that of kayaking. It's the choices we make day after day over years that can have the greatest impact on our health.

> **" I WANTED TO ENCOURAGE PADDLERS TO WORK TOWARD ALIGNMENT AND BALANCE USING YOGA AS A PREVENTIVE MEASURE.**

Incorporating a yoga for paddling practice into your health routine can help you balance the imbalances in your body, prevent injury, and paddle comfortably for many years to come. However, it's also important to understand that you can injure yourself in yoga just as you can injure yourself paddling. As I mentioned earlier, it's not just about what we do, but how we do it. Similar to what the yoga teacher in the *Sports Illustrated* article emphasized, if we practice yoga and move without an awareness of our imbalances, then we continue to exacerbate and train those imbalances. The stronger the imbalances in our bodies, the higher the risk for injury. That's why I'm including anatomy and alignment chapters in this book—to help the reader grow their knowledge and understanding of optimal alignment, and then apply that knowledge to paddling and yoga.

The attitude of the practitioner toward their yoga practice, and activities in general, also matters when it comes to injury prevention. Pushing too hard in an activity without any regard for the warning signs of the body's natural intelligence can lead to greater risk of injury. The same is true in yoga.

The yoga in this book isn't about approaching the poses as a workout or getting the deepest stretch possible. In fact, it's important to know that yoga is not about being flexible, and that you don't need to be flexible to do yoga. Come to yoga just as you are. The more you practice, the more comfortable you'll become and the more benefit you'll receive. It's just like paddling. You didn't paddle like the best paddlers in the world when you started (and perhaps still don't), but that didn't/doesn't stop you from paddling and enjoying the sport. We all start somewhere. In yoga for paddling we are focused on cultivating strength, suppleness, and balance in our bodies, not achieving some pretzel-like posture that you've seen in books and magazines or on social media.

Paul Villecourt

CHAPTER **2**

ANATOMY OF PADDLING

MY PHYSICAL THERAPIST/YOGA THERAPIST says that every muscle in the body has a dream of being strong *and* supple for optimal performance. Muscles want to be able to produce force when called into action and be able to yield when it's time to stretch and relax. Unfortunately, our daily activities often thwart that dream by chronically contracting some muscles, leaving others underactive and sleepy.

Take the shoulders, pectorals, and upper back as an example. A paddler's pectorals and the fronts of the shoulders are overused in the motion of forward paddling, causing them to be chronically contracted. When the muscles on one side of the body are chronically shortened, it usually means that the muscles on the other side of the body are underactive. In this case, if there is no countermovement to strengthen the muscles of the upper back (rhomboids, middle and upper trapezius and erector spinae), it leaves the upper back unable to draw the shoulders back into optimal alignment. This misalignment can lead to rotator cuff tears and other shoulder problems such as trigger points and muscle spasms in the shoulder blade area.

Think of your musculoskeletal system as one system linked by connective tissue. Just as individual waves are part of the ocean and have an impact on the entire sea, so do individual muscles have an impact on the function of the entire body. This is an important concept to understand for healing our bodies, reducing the risk of injury, and achieving optimal performance. If you don't understand

Opposite: Paddling in the blue waters of Luke Jocassee, South Carolina

the currents in the ocean and how they work together, then it's difficult to perform maneuvers such as paddling out past the break efficiently.

A similar analogy could be made with a river. In order to peel out of an eddy, you need to understand the downstream current, the eddy line, the feature creating the eddy, and the current inside the eddy. It's all connected, and being able to engage when you need to engage and pause when you need to pause is important for executing a successful river running move.

Muscles are attached to tendons that are attached to bones. This means that when muscles are overused and chronically contract, they have an effect not only on other muscles but also on tendons and bones. The impact of misalignments can cause discomfort and pain in the body, and eventually lead to an increased risk of injury.

The source of pain in the body is not always obvious, and it helps to have a basic understanding of anatomy. For example, chronically contracted hip flexor muscles can pull the pelvis out of alignment, leading to back pain. In my experience, most kayakers who experience low back pain go straight to a forward fold in yoga, thinking that lengthening the low back is what's needed. Although stretching the hamstrings can be beneficial for kayakers, stretching the hip flexors is what will actually help bring the pelvis back into optimal alignment, relieving the discomfort.

> " THE SOURCE OF PAIN IN THE BODY IS NOT ALWAYS OBVIOUS, AND IT HELPS TO HAVE A BASIC UNDERSTANDING OF ANATOMY.

I suffered from trigger points in the shoulder blades mentioned above. I was sure that the knots I was feeling were due to the strength and overuse of my upper back muscles. I would try to stretch them out by taking my arm across my chest to stretch the upper back, a stretch I see paddlers doing all the time. What I didn't realize was that particular stretch exacerbated the problem by contributing to the over-lengthened state of my upper back muscles. After taking my first yoga therapy training in 2010, I became aware of the root cause of these knots. From that moment I worked to strengthen my upper back, and the trigger points disappeared. A basic understanding of anatomy, and how muscle imbalances affect our alignment, allows us to make better choices when it comes to taking care of our bodies.

The inability of just one muscle group to move through its full range of motion can have an impact on performance and comfort. For example, hamstrings must be strong enough to keep our knees bent when we sit in our kayaks or canoes or stand on our SUPs. On the other hand, they also need to be supple enough to allow us to sit or stand with our pelvis tilted forward (anterior tilt) for good posture. Good posture leads to optimal core engagement, which leads to optimal power in our strokes. Paddlers who have shortened hamstrings paddle with their low backs rounded. This position can lead to back pain, an increased risk for disk injury, and poor stroke technique.

> " BY PAYING ATTENTION TO OUR BODIES AND BRINGING BALANCE TO THE IMBALANCES, WE HAVE THE POTENTIAL TO HEAL OURSELVES BEFORE INVASIVE INTERVENTION IS NEEDED.

Strengthening the muscles that we underuse in paddling and stretching the muscles that we overuse helps to bring our bodies back into optimal alignment. Alignment can help prevent and reduce pain, discomfort, and injury. By paying attention to our bodies and bringing balance to the imbalances, we have the potential to heal ourselves before invasive intervention is needed. I do the work required to bring optimal alignment to my body so that I can continue to enjoy the sport that I love. Not only enjoy it, but paddle with skill, ease, comfort, and strength.

Optimal alignment also allows for freedom and ease of movement. Hunched shoulders, poor posture, and an inability to enjoy the sports we love does not have to be our destiny in old age. We can choose to take care of our bodies and our alignment. By doing so, we give ourselves the best possible chance of enjoying a strong, supple, and active body throughout our lives. Crucial bodily functions such as digestion, breathing, and elimination also work better with optimal alignment. Our diaphragms have room to move, and our organs don't get compressed, which can lead to reduced function. Doing the work to balance our imbalances is important, not only for our ability to paddle, but also for the state of our overall health and quality of life.

In this book I've chosen poses that focus mainly on opening the front of the body (a countermovement to paddling), as well as targeting other relevant areas, such as the hamstrings. The positioning of the poses themselves can help paddlers

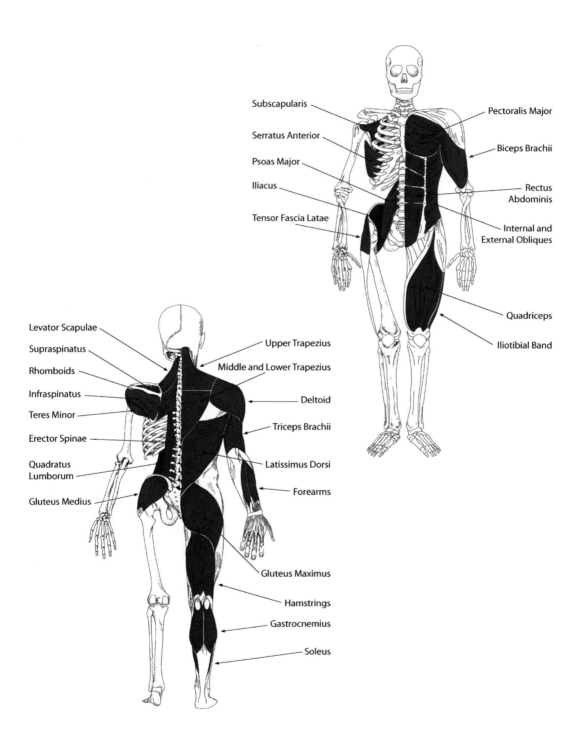

Subscapularis

Serratus Anterior

Psoas Major

Iliacus

Tensor Fascia Latae

Pectoralis Major

Biceps Brachii

Rectus Abdominis

Internal and External Obliques

Quadriceps

Iliotibial Band

Levator Scapulae

Supraspinatus

Rhomboids

Infraspinatus

Teres Minor

Erector Spinae

Quadratus Lumborum

Gluteus Medius

Upper Trapezius

Middle and Lower Trapezius

Deltoid

Triceps Brachii

Latissimus Dorsi

Forearms

Gluteus Maximus

Hamstrings

Gastrocnemius

Soleus

balance their bodies. I've also included alignment principles, subtle actions that can be engaged while in the poses. These alignment principles are covered in chapter 3.

To understand how yoga for paddling can benefit your body and performance, it's important to have a basic knowledge of the muscles we are targeting in this book. I'm not an anatomist, so my intention with this information is not to be overly detail oriented. I want to provide a big-picture view that sets the reader up for further exploration and learning. It's relatively straightforward to feel and understand the imbalances that arise from the movement of the upper body in paddling. The lower body, however, is mostly static, whether sitting, kneeling, or standing.

The muscles of the lower body engage in isometric contractions. This means the length of the muscle and the joint angle don't change. In other words, the muscles are engaging but not moving. Muscles can be complex, with anterior and posterior fibers activating in different ways during isometric contraction. It is out of the scope of this book to delve into these details. I encourage every reader who is interested in learning more about the details of the anatomy of paddling to seek out further education by scheduling a visit with a competent health professional, physical therapist, yoga therapist, and/or yoga teacher.

The diagrams on the opposite page highlight the muscles we are targeting in this book, either to strengthen or to lengthen.

Below is a brief description of the functions of the muscles highlighted in the diagrams and how they either activate or become sleepy due to the motions of paddling.

Hips and Legs

ILIACUS > The iliacus flexes the hip (brings the thigh toward the chest). This muscle is generally overused in kayaking due to the sitting position, in SUP due to hip flexion, and in canoeing due to the kneeling position. All three sports engage the iliacus in hip flexion, leading to chronic contraction.

PSOAS MAJOR > The psoas major flexes the hip and acts as a lumbar spine stabilizer. Similar to the iliacus, the psoas major is engaged in hip flexion while kayaking, canoeing, and SUPing. In kayaking and canoeing this occurs because of the seated and kneeling positions. In SUP it is due to the hip flexion required for balancing and paddling effectively. The psoas major runs from the inner thigh, across the pelvis, and attaches to the lumbar and thoracic spine. It is a major player in spine and pelvis misalignment when it becomes chronically contracted.

TENSOR FASCIA LATAE (TFL) AND IT BAND > The TFL is responsible for internal rotation, flexion, and abduction (movement away from the midline of the body) of the hip. The long tendon of this small muscle is the iliotibial band (IT band). The IT band travels from the front of the hip to the tibia just below the knee. The IT band's main function is to help stabilize the knee. Generally both the TFL and the IT band are overused in kayaking and canoeing due to the seated and kneeling positions that lead to tightening and shortening of the hip flexors. An overactive TFL combined with sleepy glutes can lead to a chronically contracted IT band. In SUP the TFL is overactive due to its tendency to compensate for knee stabilization and balance when the glutes are weak (and they usually are in most people—even those who think that they have strong glutes).

GLUTEUS MEDIUS > Gluteus medius primarily performs hip abduction. The glutes' function can be complex when it comes to isometric contraction while sitting in a kayak or canoe, or standing on a SUP. Essentially, the glutes are usually sleepy in paddlers due to the chronic contraction of the hip flexors. On a SUP, or just standing on land, if the body's center of mass rests in the ball of the foot instead of the heel, then the glutes become underused and sleepy.

GLUTEUS MAXIMUS > Gluteus maximus performs extension and external rotation of the hip. Same as with gluteus medius, the basic concept is that paddlers have sleepy glutes due to overactive hip flexors or weight bearing in the balls of the feet instead of in the heels.

QUADRICEPS > The quads are made up of four muscles in the front of the thigh. Their main function is knee extension (straightening the knee). One of these muscles, rectus femoris (the middle muscle), crosses the hip joint and also performs hip flexion. Due to the hip flexion required for sitting in a kayak and kneeling in a canoe, this muscle tends to be overactive. It is also chronically contracted in SUP paddlers due to hip flexion while balancing and paddling.

HAMSTRINGS > There are three hamstring muscles, and they all perform knee flexion and hip extension, and assist with internal and external rotation of the hip. The hamstrings become shortened due to the static position of bent knees in kayaking and canoeing. The isometric bracing that happens in the legs, mostly by pressing against the kayak's thigh braces, also contributes to shortened hamstrings. In SUP the hamstrings are contracted in a static standing position with the knees slightly bent.

CALVES > The gastrocnemius and soleus are responsible for ankle plantar flexion (rising onto your tippy-toes) and knee flexion (gastrocnemius only). They become chronically contracted during kayaking due to the action of pressing the ball of the foot into the foot pedals or bulkheads. Calves tend to be sleepy in canoeists who sit with the tops of their feet flat due to the lack of activation in that position. Canoeists who sit with their toes curled under and the balls of their feet pressed into the foot pegs will have chronically contracted calf muscles. SUP paddlers are mostly balanced, unless they have their heels lifted off the board during the propulsion phase of the forward stroke. In that case they may tend toward chronic contraction.

Shoulders, Neck, and Upper Back
DELTOID > The deltoid performs the bulk of shoulder abduction (taking arms out to the sides). It also assists with shoulder flexion and internal rotation. All the functions of this muscle are used in the motion of paddling, leading to chronic contraction.

UPPER TRAPEZIUS > The upper traps perform scapular elevation and upward rotation. Extension, lateral flexion (side bending), and rotation of the cervical spine are also part of their job. All these functions are key movements in paddling, especially one-bladed paddling such as canoeing and SUPing. It can be typical to see one trap stronger than the other, especially in canoeists who use cross-bow strokes instead of switching sides like SUP paddlers do. This creates an imbalance that can affect neck and spinal alignment over time. The traps also play a key role in the movement of performing the kayak roll (side bending).

LEVATOR SCAPULAE > Levator scapulae perform scapular elevation and lateral flexion (side bending) of the cervical spine. They are overused in the movements involved in paddling and kayak rolling.

ROTATOR CUFF > The rotator cuff includes four muscles whose primary job is to stabilize the humerus in the glenoid fossa of the scapula. Its main function is shoulder joint stability. Each of the rotator cuff muscles also plays a role in shoulder movement. The supraspinatus initiates the first 15 degrees of shoulder abduction (movement away from the center of the body). The subscapularis internally rotates the shoulder. Infraspinatus and teres minor perform external rotation of the shoulder and are more likely to be underused in paddling, which can lead to shoulder instability and injury. Rotator cuff injuries are among the most common injuries in paddlesports and can have a profound effect on a paddler's ability to continue paddling. Strengthening the infraspinatus and teres minor, along with the upper back, can contribute to shoulder stability.

MIDDLE AND LOWER TRAPEZIUS > The middle and lower trapezius perform scapular retraction and depression. These functions can counteract the upward and forward pull of the upper trapezius, which is heavily overused in paddling. Strengthening the middle and lower trapezius can help bring the shoulders and rib cage into optimal alignment.

RHOMBOIDS > Rhomboids are responsible for scapular retraction (pulling the scapula into the correct anatomical position). Because of the chronic contraction of the pectorals, the rhomboids tend to be sleepy for most paddlers. Weakened and stressed rhomboids attempting to pull the shoulders back into optimal alignment can lead to painful trigger points.

ERECTOR SPINAE > These long muscles run up and down both sides of the spine and are the major spinal extensors that hold your spine upright. Weak erector spinae can lead to impaired shoulder, scapular, and rib cage positioning. As a consequence the shoulders roll forward, and the front low ribs thrust forward to compensate. This is a common misalignment in paddlers whose shoulders are pulled forward due to chronically contracted pectorals. Strengthening the erector spinae can lead to better posture and more optimal shoulder alignment.

Chest and Arms

PECTORALIS MAJOR > Pectoralis major performs adduction (movement toward the midline of the body), horizontal adduction (bringing arms forward and inward such as when giving yourself a hug), and internal rotation of the shoulder. This muscle also assists with shoulder flexion and extension. The pectoralis major is one of the major muscles powering the forward stroke and tends to be chronically contracted, pulling the shoulders out of optimal alignment.

BICEPS BRACHII > Biceps brachii are responsible for elbow flexion, forearm supination (rotation of forearm and hand so that palms face forward or upward), and shoulder flexion. The biceps tend to be overactive in paddlers due to the elbow flexion in paddling, as well as from lifting and carrying boats and boards.

TRICEPS BRACHII > Triceps brachii perform elbow extension and shoulder extension. The triceps are more active in one-bladed paddlers who keep both, or just their top arm, extended while paddling. They are less active in kayakers, although they do play a part in the motion of the top arm pushing forward in the kayak forward stroke.

FOREARM MUSCLES > The forearm muscles include many muscles that control movements of the wrist, hand, and fingers. They are highly taxed by gripping activities such as holding a paddle, and when chronically contracted can lead to wrist problems.

Trunk/Torso

ABDOMINALS > There are four layers of anterior (front) abdominal muscles. Rectus abdominis is the most superficial abdominal muscle whose main job is trunk flexion. Kayakers and canoeists have strong abdominals, as their trunk is flexed for the motions of paddling and sitting with a slight forward lean. SUP paddlers have strong abdominals due to the mini sit-up that is performed with every forward stroke in the hinge at the hips.

INTERNAL AND EXTERNAL OBLIQUES > The intermediate layers of the obliques perform trunk flexion and rotation. Transversus abdominis is the deepest layer, and its job is simply to compress the abdominal contents and provide deep support for the spine. Effective paddling technique involves torso rotation and core engagement. The obliques are strong in paddlers who have effective technique and weak in paddlers with ineffective technique (paddling using just their arms instead of their torso).

SERRATUS ANTERIOR > The serratus anterior protracts (draws forward) the scapula, assists with scapular rotation, and keeps the scapula approximated (anchored) to the posterior chest wall. This muscle has been nicknamed "the boxer's muscle," which compares the mechanics of the "reach" in the catch phase of the forward stroke to throwing a punch. The serratus anterior allows the scapula to wrap forward toward the chest, allowing the bottom arm to reach farther forward. It's part of what we call "torso rotation" in paddling. Anytime there is a rotation of the trunk to reach the arm forward and/or across, the serratus anterior is at work. If a paddler has good paddling technique, then this muscle may be overactive.

LATISSIMUS DORSI > Latissimus dorsi performs shoulder adduction (movement toward the midline of the body), extension, and internal rotation. It's also used for extension and lateral flexion of the lumbar spine. The lats are a key muscle used in powering torso rotation in kayaking and in pressing the paddle down for canoeing and SUPing. It's key in the sweep movement of the kayak roll.

QUADRATUS LUMBORUM > This muscle laterally flexes the trunk (side bending), extends the lumbar spine, and hikes the hip. It plays a key role in the "hip snap" and in edge control in kayaking and canoeing. It is also an important muscle for stabilizing and balancing on a SUP while paddling.

SUMMARY

If this anatomy of paddling section seems like a lot of information, it is! The body is a complex and amazing machine. This chapter is not meant to be a full and complete description of the anatomy of paddling, but it provides the basics to get started. The main concepts to take away are:

- The musculoskeletal system is one system connected by connective tissue.

- Muscles are attached to tendons that are attached to bones. This means that when some muscles are chronically contracted, they can pull other muscles, tendons, and bones out of optimal alignment. In turn, this can lead to an increased risk of injury.

- The purpose of yoga for paddling is to balance the imbalances in the body that occur due to the motions and positions of paddling. This means strengthening the muscles that are underused when paddling and lengthening the muscles that are overused. Your understanding of this depends on how aware you are of your own body. Are you paddling with effective technique using your torso, or mainly muscling with your arms? If you paddle a canoe, do you sit with your feet flexed or pointed? These questions matter. I've laid out information in this chapter that I hope leads you to greater self-awareness. In turn, you can use that self-awareness, combined with the information in the rest of this book, to move your muscles through counteractions that lead to greater balance, alignment, and well-being.

Paul Villecourt

ALIGNMENT PRINCIPLES

THE POSES I'VE CHOSEN for this book target the muscle imbalances that can be caused by paddling. Going a step further, this chapter introduces alignment principles. These are subtle actions that you can perform while holding a pose that enhance the pose's effectiveness in bringing your body into optimal alignment. Optimal alignment allows you to bring steadiness and ease into each posture by balancing the imbalances in the musculoskeletal system.

These alignment principles are small adjustments. For some, they may be challenging to perform, or difficult to even feel in the body. If you've never explored alignment, it may feel very foreign. Working on alignment may make you feel as if you can't go as deep as you're accustomed to in a pose, which is entirely normal. My students often express surprise at how challenging it can be to work these principles into the poses. I've heard them say things like: "I can't believe I'm sweating so much considering that I'm not moving as much as in a flow class."

I compare the experience to a paddler who has been paddling for several years without any formal instruction and then takes a class from a competent instructor. The paddler may be so accustomed to paddling only with his or her arms that torso rotation may actually feel wrong and difficult. Your experience with alignment principles may feel similar if you've been incorporating imbalances into your yoga practice.

Opposite: Using the subtle actions of alignment principles to move toward optimal alignment while standing.

Although there are many lineages of yoga, each one offering benefits to the body, mind, and spirit, alignment-based yoga is simply the style that has worked best for healing muscle tweaks, reducing pain, and preventing paddling injuries in my body. It has also allowed me to continue to enjoy whitewater kayaking at a very active level in my forties, having spent twenty years paddling 200-plus days per year. My body has stayed strong and supple enough to take on SUP, whitewater SUP, and paddle surfing in the last six years. I'm amazed at how effective alignment-based yoga is in contributing to long-term paddling health and vitality. I invite you to explore this style of yoga and see how it feels for your body.

> " ALIGNMENT-BASED YOGA IS SIMPLY THE STYLE THAT HAS WORKED BEST FOR HEALING MUSCLE TWEAKS, REDUCING PAIN, AND PREVENTING PADDLING INJURIES IN MY BODY.

It's important to use these alignment principles in your yoga practice and when paddling, where they apply, but also while sitting, standing, and moving in your day-to-day life. Correcting your posture over and over throughout the day is what will bring the most powerful healing to your body. It is the choices that we make moment to moment, day to day, that have the biggest impact on our health and well-being.

Below are detailed explanations of the alignment principles. I've studied and taught alignment-based yoga since 2010 and have consulted with my physical therapist on these principles. In later chapters I list the pertinent principles in the directions for each pose, but I don't explain them or go into their benefits in detail like I do here, so please refer back to this section for clarity when needed. The alignment principles are designed to be used together to promote optimal alignment of the spine, rib cage, and pelvis. Once you become familiar with them, you can engage them pretty much anywhere, including while paddling, sitting at your desk, standing, and walking. The more you incorporate them into your daily life off the mat, the easier it is to train your body to come back to and maintain optimal alignment.

1. Press Through the Heels to Activate the Backs of the Legs

Shifting your body weight back so that the center of mass lands mostly over the heels activates the back body. This is different from simply leaning back. The shift happens by moving the pelvis back (different from a pelvic tilt), not leaning back. This action helps to strengthen the glutes, stabilize the knees, and increase

Chair pose with weight in balls of the feet.

Chair pose with weight in heels. Notice the stability and strength in the legs compared to the first photo.

balance. It also counteracts the chronic contraction of the hip flexors, allowing them to lengthen and give the pelvis more freedom of movement. Shifting most of your weight into your heels also allows the toes to be free to lift and spread. It's easier to see this weight shift in a pose like chair pose (see photos), though this alignment principle is performed standing.

Importance for Paddlers

Too much weight centered in the forefeet can cause irritation of the plantar fascia and toes, which can lead to foot and toe problems. Canoeists, for example, may experience arch problems due to the position of the feet in the kneeling position. This forward shift of the center of mass also shifts the pelvis out of alignment, causing all kinds of problems in the hips and low back. The heel bone is designed for weight bearing. Taking weight into the heels helps the pelvis stack over the long bones of the legs and in turn leads to increased ability to achieve optimal alignment.

This alignment principle is especially important for SUP paddlers who stand while paddling. Increased balance, knee stability, alignment, and strength will lead to better and more enjoyable paddling. It's also an important countermovement to the chronic contraction of the hip flexors in all the paddling disciplines. Striking a balance between the glutes and the hip flexors can take pressure off muscles like the TFL, including the IT band, and allow them to soften. This in turn can help to reduce pain and tightness in the fronts and sides of the legs as well as the low back.

How to Do This Action

Stand with your feet sitz bones (see alignment principle #3) distance apart and parallel to each other. Take a moment to stand tall and shift your center of gravity forward into the balls of your feet and then back into your heels. Do this back and forth a few times. Notice the difference between the muscles that activate in your legs when your weight is shifted into the balls of your feet versus the ones that activate when your heels are bearing most of the weight.

Next, soften your knees and, moving from the pelvis, shift your weight back until you feel that the backs of your legs are engaged all the way up to your glutes. Even though your center of mass is now over your heels, you should still be able to comfortably press the balls of your feet into the ground for stability. Press strongly into the heels as if you were growing roots from the bottoms of your heels into the floor. Lift and spread your toes while keeping the balls of your feet pressing down, and then place them back on the ground spread and activated.

2. Soft Knees

Hyperextension of the knees weakens the joint and surrounding ligaments and can lead to knee instability and lack of range of motion. Keeping a slight bend in the knees helps to keep the joint and ligaments strong and the knees stable.

Importance for Paddlers

"Soft knees" is a cue I use when teaching SUP for greater stability and shock absorption while paddling. Hyperextended knees (on land or on a SUP) can create misalignment all the way up through the spine. Standing with soft knees also reduces stress on the joint itself. For canoeists, who tend toward knee problems

Hyperextended knees.

Standing with soft knees protects the surrounding tissue and ligaments and has a positive effect on the alignment of the pelvis.

due to the kneeling position, this can be an important aspect of body awareness for knee health.

How to Do This Action

Standing with your feet parallel and sitz bones distance apart, become aware of the position of your knees. If they are pressed back and locked out, soften your knees by bending them slightly. I consistently bring awareness to my knees and how I'm standing throughout the day and in my yoga practice. The combination of weight in the heels and soft knees should create a feeling of stability and strength in your lower body.

I've witnessed students resist keeping their knees soft in yoga poses because they have the idea that good yogis keep their knees straight. The incredibly flexible people doing extreme versions of yoga poses seen in print and social media are usually hypermobile. Being hypermobile may look cool in a photo, but over time can lead to joint and alignment problems. Some practitioners have also heard the cue "straighten the knees" in yoga classes. Again, there is no right or wrong. But to get the most out of this particular style of yoga, and keeping in line with the intentions of this book, we'll focus on keeping a slight bend in the knees while practicing.

3. Take Your Sitz Bones Back and Apart

Your sitz bones, or ischial tuberosities, are the pointy bones in your butt cheeks that you sit on. When you actively take them back and apart, you tilt your pelvis anteriorly (forward). This means that if your pelvis were a bowl filled with water, it is tilted such that the water gently pours out onto the floor in front of you. This is how your pelvis wants to sit. The key is to initiate this movement with your sitz bones, not your low back (low back activation can lead to too much anterior tilt). When activated, this principle releases hip flexors, restores lumbar curvature, promotes length in the spine, and reduces back pain. It also tones the lower abdominal muscles. It does require some hamstring flexibility.

Importance for Paddlers

This alignment principle will have a specific effect on the posture of each paddler depending on which discipline they practice. Let's go through each.

Taking the sitz bones back and apart leads to an anterior tilt of the pelvis.

A posterior tilt of the pelvis can lead to increased risk of injury and back pain.

Kayaking

Sitting in a kayak with legs apart and externally rotated, while also engaging the inner thighs in the thigh braces, can lead to rounding of the low back. My PT calls this "sacral sitting"—when we sit on the lower part of the sacrum rather than on the sitz bones. Over time, sitting with the pelvis tilted posteriorly (holding the water in the pelvic bowl instead of pouring it forward onto the floor) leads to low back pain and injury, including lumbar disk herniations. Taking the sitz bones back and apart works to counteract the rounding of the low back and establishes a neutral pelvis as the foundation for the spine, so the spine can be free. This allows kayakers to sit up tall, which is the foundation for effective kayaking technique.

Canoeing

Kneeling in a canoe actually makes it easier to tilt the pelvis anteriorly (so that water pours out the front). In fact, canoeists should be very aware of the curvature of their lumbar spines. It may be that any imbalance that they experience is from too much anterior tilt of the pelvis. If engaging this alignment principle feels like crunching in the low back, then focus on lengthening the sitz bones down (pressing them into the floor) instead of back and apart. This will give length to the low back.

Canoeists who have tight hamstrings are more prone to rounding of the low back, and the cues of "back" and "apart" can be beneficial. It can help to look in the mirror from the side and determine if your low back is rounded or arched. I also recommend bringing awareness to how the low back and pelvis feel while sitting in your canoe. This is where a book cannot do the job as effectively as an experienced yoga teacher. Having said that, bringing attention to your pelvic area with this alignment principle is a good beginning to increased body awareness.

SUP

When paddlers stand on their SUPs, the imbalances and related compensations in their bodies become very obvious. Muscles must work harder to balance and stabilize on a SUP, leading to further chronic contraction in the most powerful muscles, like the hip flexors. Taking the sitz bones back and apart, while shifting the center of mass into the heels to engage the glutes, allows the hip flexors to lengthen. This principle can be very beneficial for SUP paddlers.

In a similar vein as kayaking, SUP paddlers who paddle with their pelvis tilted posteriorly increase their risk for back pain and injury. A posteriorly tilted pelvis also makes it harder to balance and rotate the core. The hinge at the hips, a key component of a powerful forward stroke on a SUP, will happen more easily and with more power when the sitz bones are back and apart.

I've also seen SUP paddlers with too much anterior tilt in their pelvis develop low back pain. As mentioned above in the paragraph for canoeists, check your alignment in a mirror, and if you see exaggerated anterior tilt, focus on pressing the sitz bones down toward the board or floor instead of back and apart.

How to Do This Action

At first it's a good idea to become familiar with this action by sitting cross-legged, reaching back, and manually moving the flesh out from under your sitz bones. You should feel a shift from sitting on the back of your sitz bones to sitting on the front of your sitz bones. Your pelvis should be tilted anteriorly (so that water pours out the front onto the floor). You'll notice that you can sit up taller and

that your thighs and knees will lift slightly. You may need to sit on a few folded blankets if your hips and hamstrings are chronically tight. Don't be afraid to use blankets to help you sit up! I always sit on blankets for meditation. I would rather work toward optimal alignment with the help of blankets than be stubborn and suffer from imbalances.

Another way to engage this action is to think of pressing the sitz bones into the floor to sit up taller (thinking of pressing them down can also bring them back and apart). Once you are familiar with what this feels like in a seated position, you can perform the action in other poses. Keeping soft knees, or knees slightly bent, also gives the pelvis more freedom to tilt anteriorly.

4. Take the Front Low Ribs Down, Expand the Back Ribs, and Lengthen the Upper Spine

This cue is a mouthful, and it's important. Most of us sit with our pelvis posteriorly tilted (low back rounded as discussed above) and our front ribs jutting forward. When we perform torso rotation with our front ribs jutting forward, we create a shearing action at the thoraco-lumbar junction. This shearing can lead to wear and tear in that area, back pain, and tension in the quadratus lumborum and psoas major (hip flexors). It can also cause injury over time. When you take the front low ribs back, expand the back ribs, and lengthen through the upper spine,

Standing with ribs thrusting forward.

Standing taking the low front ribs back, expanding the back ribs, and lengthening through the spine. The difference is subtle and a work in progress.

you bring your thoracic spine toward optimal alignment. This action strengthens the erector spinae, which helps to draw the shoulders back into an optimal position. It reduces shearing at the thoraco-lumbar junction, allows for stronger torso rotation, reduces back pain, and helps to protect the rotator cuff.

Importance for Paddlers
The benefits mentioned above are consistent for kayakers, canoeists, and SUP paddlers. The major benefit is protection of the rotator cuff and reduction of shearing at the thoraco-lumbar junction.

How to Do This Action
First, notice if your ribs are jutting forward. Draw your front low ribs toward your back ribs. Place your hands on your front ribs if this helps you initiate the movement. As you move your front ribs toward your back ribs, you'll notice that

Back bend initiated by thrusting the rib cage forward.

Back bend initiated using this alignment principle. Notice the length created and maintained in the low and mid back.

your back ribs naturally expand. Next, lengthen through the upper spine and out the crown of the head without letting your front ribs jut forward again. It can be a challenge to engage this alignment principle while keeping the sitz bones back and apart. You may notice that as you bring your front low ribs down, your pelvis also wants to tilt posteriorly. Try to keep your sitz bones back and apart while you take your front low ribs down, expand the back ribs, and lengthen through the upper spine. Now we're getting somewhere! You should feel a subtle lengthening of the low back when both principles are engaged.

I cue this alignment principle in back bends, which may be surprising. We'll be entering into back bends without thrusting our front ribs forward. If you're a seasoned practitioner, it may change the feel of a back bend, and I invite you to explore the benefits. Even though it may initially keep you from going as deep as you usually do in a back bend, it will help to maintain length in the low back, support alignment of the rib cage, and create spaciousness in your torso. The idea is to lengthen first before dropping into back bends.

5. Draw the Shoulder Blades Back and Down

This action increases scapular stability by strengthening the muscles surrounding the scapula. In turn, this helps to protect the rotator cuff. It's a counteraction to the forward pull on the shoulders and chronically contracted pectoral muscles.

Shoulders rolled forward.

Shoulder position where shoulder blades are back and down.

Importance for Paddlers
This action is important for the shoulder health and stability of all paddlers, no matter the craft.

How to Do This Action
Squeeze the shoulder blades back and toward each other. Next, slide them down the back so they feel integrated onto your back body. This principle is fairly easy to activate; however, the challenge is to perform this action while maintaining

Spider cobra with the shoulders rolled forward.

Spider cobra with the shoulders blades back and down, allowing for an extension through the chest and a strengthening of the upper back and shoulder girdle.

the previous alignment principles, including keeping your front low ribs from jutting forward.

6. Spread Your Fingers Wide, and Press Your Fingertip Pads and the Balls of Your Index Fingers into the Floor

This alignment principle is engaged in poses that require taking weight into the hands. It takes the weight of the body out of the heel of the hand and distributes it throughout the hand. Instead of attempting to balance on one point of the hand, weight is distributed and stabilized through the entire hand.

Importance for Paddlers

Wrist health, stability, and function are key for paddlers. This alignment principle helps to keep your wrists functional on and off the water. The combination of lots of paddling and a lack of awareness of effective weight distribution through the hands during yoga practice can lead to wrist pain. Paddlers already put strain on their wrists when they paddle, and to maintain long-term function it's important to be kind to them off the water.

How to Do This Action

Think of a tripod. Without the legs of the tripod extended, it can't balance and hold weight. Once the legs of the tripod are extended, they help to distribute weight evenly for stability. Engage your fingertip pads and the balls of your index fingers like the legs of a tripod for even weight distribution. When engaged properly, the heel of the hand will feel light and slightly lifted off the floor, and there will be space between the middle of the palm and the floor.

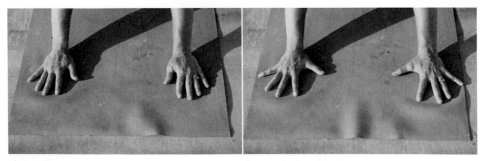

Hands that aren't activated can put a lot of pressure on the wrists.

Engaging the hands takes pressure off the wrists.

SUMMARY

The poses I've chosen for this book strengthen the muscles that are underused in paddling and lengthen the muscles that are overused. In addition, you can choose to engage alignment principles while holding the poses.

- The alignment principles are subtle actions.

- They can enhance the poses' effectiveness in balancing imbalances caused by paddling.

- They enhance body awareness.

- The alignment principles are meant to be used together for optimal effect on alignment.

- These alignment principles can be used in yoga practice, when paddling (when appropriate), and in day-to-day activities such as driving a car and standing in line.

THE BREATH AND STRESS REDUCTION

BREATHWORK (PRANAYAMA) IS ONE of the eight limbs of yoga. According to yoga, the breath is our life force (prana) and can be manipulated to warm us up, cool us down, stimulate digestion, energize us, or induce relaxation. For the purpose of this book, I'm focusing on the benefits of breath control to bring you to present moment awareness in your yoga practice, and to manage the effects of stress.

Many Americans live in a constant state of stress that wreaks havoc on their health and well-being. According to the Benson-Henry Institute for Mind Body Medicine, stress-induced illnesses account for 60 to 90 percent of doctor's visits in the United States.[6] The benefits of breathwork on stress management have become increasingly well known in our culture in recent years.

Many of you reading this book have probably used paddling as an effective form of stress management. The breath is the cheapest form of stress management, and it's always available—on and off the water. According to yoga, it is a direct vehicle to the present moment, allowing all other thoughts, worries, and anxieties to fall away.

Interestingly, just because our bodies breathe naturally and unconsciously all the time doesn't mean that we breathe optimally all the time. A basic understanding of the anatomy and mechanics of breathing can help you to optimize your breath and manipulate it for different effects on the body and mind.

Opposite: Sitting with the breath
at Folly Beach, South Carolina.

Breathing Basics

Breathing has two phases, inhalation and exhalation. During inhalation the diaphragm contracts and moves down. The intercostal muscles between the ribs also contract and move the rib cage up and out, expanding the chest cavity. These movements of the diaphragm and rib cage increase the volume of the lungs (they get bigger), which in turn decreases the pressure inside the lungs (think more space, less air). Since air flows toward areas of low pressure, it flows into the lungs during inhalation. This means that we don't actually pull air into our lungs; instead, the air outside our bodies pushes its way into our lungs upon inhalation. The first time I heard this in a yoga anatomy workshop, it blew my mind. How fascinating to contemplate that I had lived thirty-five years in my body without truly understanding how breathing works!

During exhalation the body eliminates the waste product of carbon dioxide from the lungs. In this phase of breathing, the diaphragm releases and moves up into the chest cavity, and the rib cage retracts, pushing the air out of the lungs.

> **HOW FASCINATING TO CONTEMPLATE THAT I HAD LIVED THIRTY-FIVE YEARS IN MY BODY WITHOUT TRULY UNDERSTANDING HOW BREATHING WORKS!**

In terms of function, the diaphragm has the same dream as every other muscle in the body, to be able to activate when it's called into play and to yield when it's time to relax. Both functions are crucial for optimal breathing. If there are imbalances in the surrounding connective tissue, or misalignments of the rib cage, spine, and/or pelvis that don't allow the diaphragm to fully contract, the volume of the lungs doesn't change as much. The result is that less air enters the lungs.

Oxygen is nutrition for every cell in the body. Through oxidation our cells metabolize food, turning it into the energy we need to function. Cell regeneration, nutrition, and waste elimination require oxygen, which means that human life requires oxygen. Just as it is possible to starve ourselves by not ingesting enough food, so too is it possible to starve ourselves by not taking in enough oxygen. According to yoga, when we breathe in air and oxygen, we also breathe in prana (life force).

If the diaphragm isn't able to fully release due to imbalances and misalignments, the carbon dioxide (waste) may not get fully eliminated from the lungs.

According to yoga and Ayurveda, complete elimination of waste from the body is a key factor in health and well-being. Just as we don't allow waste to accumulate in our house by taking out the trash, we need to eliminate our bodies' trash so that it doesn't build up and lead to health problems. The breath and how we breathe, according to yoga, contributes to, or detracts from, the strength, vitality, and longevity of our life force.

The Breath and Stress

Stress isn't necessarily a bad thing. As a whitewater paddler and former competitor, stress is part of my paddling experience. Without some stress we don't grow and develop. One of my favorite quotes is by author Cynthia Occelli: "For a seed to achieve its greatest expression, it must come completely undone. The shell cracks, its insides come out and everything changes. To someone who doesn't understand growth, it would look like complete destruction."

In her 2013 TED talk, health psychologist Kelly McGonigal explains how stress cannot simply be labeled as bad. She uses scientific evidence to show that our attitude toward stress is a more potent factor than stress itself in determining whether or not the stress response is harmful to our health. She goes on to say that viewing the stress response as our body's way of helping us rise to face a challenge can lead to healthier stress management.

From my perspective as a whitewater enthusiast, this makes a lot of sense. In my experience, whitewater paddlers don't seem to suffer health problems from the stress of challenging themselves on rivers, but instead thrive on it. Perhaps this is because we view it as part of the experience, and as part of the eventual joy we feel at the bottom of a challenging rapid. Something similar happens in competition. Stress can be a great contributor to high performance in sports, depending on how the athlete views and manages stress.

Having said all that, studies do show that prolonged, unchecked stress can suppress the immune system, wreak havoc on our adrenal glands, increase blood pressure, and lead to anxiety and

> " PROLONGED, UNCHECKED STRESS CAN SUPPRESS THE IMMUNE SYSTEM, WREAK HAVOC ON OUR ADRENAL GLANDS, INCREASE BLOOD PRESSURE, AND LEAD TO ANXIETY AND DEPRESSION.

depression. When our sympathetic nervous system activates the stress response, stress hormones flood our bodies. Some stress hormones, such as cortisol, hang out in the body for days after the initial stress response.

Hormones are chemical messengers in the body that control major bodily functions. When we experience a chronic state of stress, due either to physical or psychological factors, stress hormones stay in constant circulation in our bodies. As they circulate, they tell our bodies that danger is always looming. If the body thinks that it is under constant threat, then it pulls energy away from vital functions such as appetite, digestion, and reproduction. There's a saying among Ayurvedic practitioners: "We are what we digest." The digestive system is responsible for transforming our food into nutrients for our cells, which in turn build our bodily tissues. When we experience poor digestion, we can experience poor tissue quality in bones, organs, muscles, and skin. That's why it's important to "rest and digest."

Scientific studies have shown that deep, slow breathing can elicit a relaxation response in the body and help activate the parasympathetic nervous system. This system is responsible for homeostasis (state of equilibrium) in the body, with one of its main functions being rest and digestion. The body enjoys, and is always trying to get back to, homeostasis, and we can help the process through breathwork.

> " SCIENTIFIC STUDIES HAVE SHOWN THAT DEEP, SLOW BREATHING CAN ELICIT A RELAXATION RESPONSE IN THE BODY AND HELP ACTIVATE THE PARASYMPATHETIC NERVOUS SYSTEM.

From the perspective of yoga, focusing on the breath brings us to present-moment awareness, interrupting the incessant flow of thoughts in the mind. When we create space between our thoughts, it then becomes possible to realize that we are not our thoughts. We are not the stories that we tell ourselves about what is happening in our lives. This helps to create the space needed for self-inquiry into who we really are beyond the machinations of the mind.

Breath awareness allows us to respond to our lives from a deeper place of calm, compassion, and authenticity, rather than reacting out of emotion, ego, and drama.

Related to paddling, an example I use is my experience of being at the top of a challenging rapid. My stress response is activated, adrenaline is pumping through my system, and my heart rate is up. The first thoughts racing through my mind are scenarios of what could go wrong. That's what our brains have evolved to do, assess the scene for threats and opportunities. Unless I have a tool that can help me pause and switch my thought patterns from negative, to affirming and confidence building, then my reaction will come from a place of fear. Taking deep, steady, full breaths is a tool that helps me to see the opportunities despite the stress. It breaks up the mental chatter so I can remember that I have skill, I can see my line, and I trust myself.

Mindful breathing nourishes our cells with prana, breaks up our thought patterns, and helps us to manage stress. Having the ability to bring steadiness and ease to yoga poses also requires breath awareness and control. It's always there and available, so why wouldn't we use it?

Belly Breathing

When the diaphragm lowers, it pushes the abdominal cavity out so that it bulges forward. Leslie Kaminoff, author of *Yoga Anatomy*, describes it like this: "The abdominal cavity changes shape like a flexible, fluid-filled structure such as a water balloon. When you squeeze one end of a water balloon, the other end bulges."[7]

Belly breathing has less to do with our bellies and more to do with the diaphragm. A bulging belly on the inhalation can mean that our diaphragm has good range of motion and function. Having said that, it is possible to breathe fully using the diaphragm effectively without bulging the belly. This is called chest breathing, and we won't go into that technique in this book. There is a common misunderstanding that if your belly doesn't bulge then the diaphragm isn't being used. This isn't the case.

The diaphragm is the muscle responsible for breathing, whether it's contracting and pushing the belly out or contracting and expanding the rib cage. There is, however, a difference between effective chest breathing and trying to keep your belly sucked in

In the ancient text called Yoga Sutras, Patanjali writes, "Sthira Sukham Asanam." My favorite translation of this is that every yoga pose (asana) should have the qualities of steadiness (sthira) and ease (sukham). Both qualities are equally important to cultivate in your practice.

while you breathe so that it appears you have a flat stomach. Doing this can hinder your ability to breathe and take in air and prana.

There are many different breath exercises in the yogic tradition, and some of them require years of study and practice under a competent teacher. For the sake of this book, we will focus on simple belly breathing. It is a good starting point to experience effective breathing, stress reduction, and present moment awareness in our yoga practice. I highly recommend consulting with a competent and experienced yoga teacher and/or Ayurvedic practitioner for training in more advanced breathwork techniques (pranayama).

Three-Count Belly Breathing

Let's start with three-count breathing, which helps to bring the inhalation and exhalation into balance by making them the same length.

- Sit in a comfortable cross-legged position. Prop yourself up on some blankets so that you can sit comfortably for several minutes (sitz bones on the blankets, feet crossed on the floor).

- Reach back and take the flesh out from under your sitz bones. Press them down into the blanket to lift up through the spine and sit tall.

- Take the front low ribs down and expand the back ribs, lifting through the upper spine and out the crown of the head.

- Place your hands on your belly.

- Inhale slowly and deeply as you count one, two, three, feeling the belly bulge out.

- Exhale slowly and completely as you count three, two, one, feeling the belly retract.

- Repeat for five breath cycles, breathing deeply, slowly, and with a steady count.

- After you've done five repetitions, take a moment to notice how you feel in your body and in your mind.

- Place your hands on your rib cage.

- Inhale slowly and deeply, focusing on and feeling the expansion of your rib cage as you count one, two, three. Your belly will also bulge. Allow it to do so while you maintain awareness on the rib cage.

- Exhale slowly and completely as you count three, two, one, feeling your ribs retract.

- Repeat for five breath cycles, breathing deeply, slowly, and with a steady count.

- After you've done five repetitions, take a moment to notice how you feel in your body and in your mind.

- Place your hands on your collarbone.

- Inhale slowly and deeply as you count one, two, three, feeling the rise of the collarbone beneath your hands. Allow your belly to bulge and your rib cage to expand as you maintain awareness on your collarbones.

- Exhale slowly and completely as you count three, two, one, feeling the fall of the collarbone beneath your hands.

- Repeat for five breath cycles, breathing deeply, slowly, and with a steady count.

- After you've done five repetitions, take a moment to notice how you feel in your body and in your mind.

Now incorporate all three of these areas in the torso into one breath cycle.

- Sit in a comfortable cross-legged position. Prop yourself up on some blankets so that you can sit comfortably for several minutes.

- Reach back and take the flesh out from under your sitz bones. Press them down into the blankets to lift up through the spine and sit tall.

- Take the front low ribs down and expand the back ribs, lifting through the upper spine and out the crown of the head.

- Place your hands comfortably on your thighs, palms up or down.

- Inhale into the belly, and feel the belly bulge.

- Draw the same breath up into your rib cage and feel the rib cage expand.

- Continue to draw the breath up into your collarbone and feel it lift (this is the most subtle of the actions).

- Exhale, and feel your belly retract.

- Continue your exhalation and feel your rib cage retract.

The second sutra in the Yoga Sutras by Patanjali is "Yogas citta vrtti nirodhah." My favorite translation is "Yoga is the cessation of the fluctuations of the mind." It's not about how difficult a pose you can do, but about how you use the pose, simple or complex, to quiet your mind. When the mind is quiet, there is nothing. Out of nothing, anything is possible.

- Complete your exhale as you feel your collarbone fall.

- Repeat—inhale into the belly, draw the breath up into the front ribs and then all the way to the collarbone.

- Exhale; belly, rib cage, collarbone.

- Inhale one, two, three.

- Exhale three, two, one.

- Keep the same three count on the inhale as on the exhale.

- Repeat for five breath cycles, breathing deeply, slowly, and with a steady count.

- After you've done five repetitions, take a moment to notice how you feel in your body and in your mind.

Keep the count steady, and make the inhalations and exhalations the same length. You can use this technique lying on the floor in a comfortable position for deeper relaxation. Bring this breath awareness and technique into the poses as your foundation. Steady, easeful breathing contributes to steadiness and ease in the poses. You can also make your breath feel more like a wave rising and falling in your body by exhaling and allowing the collarbone to drop first, then feeling the rib cage and finally the belly retract. Yoga is about self-inquiry and self-knowledge. The more you practice and explore, the more awareness opens up.

One of my favorite meditation techniques is from the Zen Master Thich Nhat Hanh. Sitting tall, say the following mantra to yourself as you inhale: "Inhaling I breathe in." As you exhale, say to yourself: "Exhaling I breathe out." Repeat this mantra over and over, coordinating the words with the breath. The mantra helps to bring you to the present moment and leads your mind toward stillness.

Pause

Once you become comfortable with maintaining inhalations and exhalations of equal length, you can start pausing for a moment at the top of the inhalation and at the bottom of the exhalation. This would look like inhale one, two, three, pause; exhale three, two, one, pause; and so on. This technique can bring more awareness to the breath and more spaciousness to the mind, and help us to delve deeper into the space of self-awareness.

Elongating the Exhalation for Deeper Relaxation

As I hope you've felt, simply bringing an awareness to the breath and making your inhalations and exhalations the same length is calming. Let's next explore how to manipulate the breath to induce even more relaxation by making your exhalation longer than your inhalation.

- Sit in a comfortable cross-legged position. Prop yourself up on some blankets so that you can sit comfortably for several minutes.

- Reach back and take the flesh out from under your sitz bones. Press them down into the blankets to lift up through the spine and sit tall.

- Take the front low ribs down and expand the back ribs, lifting through the upper spine and out the crown of the head.

- Inhale slowly and deeply, counting one, two, three.

- Exhale slowly and completely, counting four, three, two, one.

- Inhale slowly and deeply, counting one, two, three.

- Exhale slowly and completely, counting five, four, three, two, one.

- Inhale slowly and deeply, counting one, two three.

- Exhale slowly and completely, counting six, five, four, three, two, one.

- Repeat five rounds with a three-count on the inhale and a six-count on the exhale.

- Start decreasing the count on the exhalation until you come back to three counts on the inhale and three counts on the exhale.

- When you're done, take a moment to notice how you feel in your body and in your mind.

The beauty of the breath is that you can turn to it anytime. It is always available and accessible, whether you're at the top of a challenging rapid, paddling in open water, surfing a wave, or sitting in traffic in your car. It is a powerful tool for enhancing your yoga practice and paddling performance, as well as for general stress management. These breathing exercises will benefit your body and mind on and off the water.

SUMMARY

According to yoga, our breath can be manipulated for heightened present moment awareness. Effective breathing allows us to take in prana (life force) to nourish our cells and expels waste from our bodies. It is the cheapest and most accessible way to reduce stress and greatly enhances our yoga practice.

- Start with belly breathing, allowing your belly to bulge on the inhale and retract on the exhale.

- Use three-count breathing to make your inhalations and exhalations the same length.

- Pause at the top of your inhalations and the bottom of your exhalations for deeper relaxation and a sense of spaciousness.

- Make your exhalations longer than your inhalations for deeper relaxation.

- Turn to your breath on your mat, on the water, or whenever you need to reduce stress, relax, create space between your thoughts, or enjoy the moment.

Greeting the day with mindfulness.

PROPS AND SELF-CARE

I WANT TO INTRODUCE YOGA PROPS so that you know they are available to support your body in the poses. This book could potentially be 500 pages long if I were to include all the different variations in poses that are possible with prop assistance. Some yoga teachers feel strongly about the benefits of props. Other teachers feel strongly that using props bypasses the development of strength and length needed to move toward the full expression of a pose.

The props that I use in this book consist of blankets, a bolster, blocks, sandbags, and a strap. These props are easy to find at your local yoga shop, yoga studio, or online. I give direction on how to use these props in some of the pose descriptions, but not all of them. I use them mainly in chapter 12 (for supported relaxation poses). Most teachers are in agreement that props are wonderful tools when it comes to restorative and relaxation poses.

Don't be afraid to use props if you feel that your body needs them to feel more supported and relaxed in a pose. Almost everyone needs to sit on a few folded blankets to feel comfortable in a cross-legged position. (When using blankets I recommend folding them mindfully and cleanly so that they provide an even surface to sit on.) In my experience as a yoga practitioner and teacher, I've witnessed people in yoga class reject props because they feel that it is a sign of weakness or being "bad" at yoga. If you feel this way, recognize that it is a story you're telling yourself that isn't true. It's a construct of the ego mind that likes to judge and label things as good, bad, acceptable, not acceptable, and so on. Yoga asks us: "Can you put your ego aside and be with the moment just as it is?"

Opposite: Supported relaxation.

In our ambitious, competitive culture, we like to think that yoga is about what the postures look like, but as we've already discussed, there's a lot more to it. Are you feeling steady and at ease in the shape you're holding, whatever it looks like? Is your breathing slow, deep, and steady? Is your mind calm? If using a block, blanket, bolster, or strap helps with any of this, then allow yourself to surrender and meet your body at its capacity in that moment.

My last recommendation is to let go of comparing yourself to others and do what's best for you. One of the greatest benefits of the yogic and Ayurvedic paths for me is self-knowledge. Self-knowledge has given me the confidence to honor my unique path through life. My body is unique, my personality is unique, and my life is unique. It takes a lot more courage to recognize and choose what's right for you, than to strive for something because that's what everyone else is doing or wants you to do. If you experience any pain in your body while practicing the poses or alignment principles in this book, please stop your practice and seek out the expertise of a competent yoga teacher or health care practitioner. Learn to listen to your body's messages so that you do what is best for you and your health. It is also wise to consult a medical professional before incorporating yoga into your health or fitness routine.

> " DON'T BE AFRAID TO USE PROPS IF YOU FEEL THAT YOUR BODY NEEDS THEM TO FEEL MORE SUPPORTED AND RELAXED IN A POSE.

WARM-UPS

MINDFULLY HEATING UP THE BODY increases circulation to the muscles. This in turn allows the muscles to stretch and strengthen more effectively during your yoga practice and/or your paddling session. My favorite warm-ups are joint rotations and sun salutations.

In my personal practice I start with joint rotations, followed by three to six rounds of sun salutations, before moving into other poses. Choose to either let your body flow through the movements, or bring some alignment into each pose with the help of the alignment principles covered in chapter 3. When I'm pressed for time in the morning, practicing three to six rounds allows me to fit in an abbreviated practice.

Joint Warm-Up

Rotating the joints helps increase lubrication and maintain range of motion. It also assists with flexibility and stability and can help to prevent injury. All this is important for all types of paddlers. Ankle and knee rotations can be especially helpful to canoeists who put a lot of strain on those joints due to the kneeling position. Moving through joint rotations before you get in your boat is a wonderful way to warm up the body before paddling.

Opposite: Basking in the warmth of the setting sun at Kiawah Island, South Carolina.

ANKLE ROLLING

> Lift the heel of your left foot and rotate your ankle clockwise eight times while keeping your toes on the floor. Switch direction and rotate counterclockwise eight times. Switch feet and repeat.

NECK/HEAD ROLLING

> Initiate the head movement by drawing circles with your nose in a clockwise direction eight times. Switch directions and repeat eight times. This movement warms up the joint between the head and the neck.

SHOULDER ROLLING

> Roll your shoulders back, down, forward, and up for eight repetitions. Be sure to move the shoulders through the full range of motion even if you're just focusing on one direction.

> Switch directions and roll your shoulders forward, down, back, and up eight times using your full range of motion.

TORSO TWISTING

> Stand with feet just outside hip width and rotate the torso left, then right, allowing your arms to swing with the rotation. You can let your front hand hit your body just below your collarbone, and your back hand can tap the low back. This movement is energizing and warms up the torso.

> Exhale as you twist left, and inhale as you twist right.

> One full rotation (left and right) is considered one movement. Repeat eight times.

HIP ROTATIONS/CIRCLES

> Make big circles with your hips, moving them to one side and forward, then to the other side and back.

> Repeat eight times.

> Do eight rotations in the other direction.

FLEXION AND EXTENSION OF THE SPINE

> Place your hands on your thighs. On an inhale, soften between your shoulder blades, take your sitz bones back, bend your knees deeply, and look up.

> On an exhale, round the back and tuck the chin, pressing the upper back toward the ceiling. Repeat eight times.

> This movement feels like an African dance move and takes the spine through flexion and extension.

KNEE ROTATIONS/CIRCLES

> Bring your feet and knees together.

> Bend your knees and place your hands on your thighs.

> Circle your knees together as a unit eight times in one direction.

> Switch directions for eight circles.

WRIST ROTATIONS/FIGURE EIGHTS

> Clasp your hands together in front of your chest.

> Roll your wrists as a unit in a figure-eight pattern eight times in one direction.

> Switch directions for eight rotations.

SUN SALUTATIONS

Sun salutations start and end in mountain pose, a foundation pose in yoga. This is a great pose to practice the alignment principles from chapter 3.

> Stand at the front of your mat with your feet parallel and sitz bones distance apart. Bend your knees slightly and take your sitz bones back and apart. Invite your front low ribs down and expand your back ribs. Lengthen up and out the crown of the head.

> Shift your weight so that your heels are weighted and the backs of your legs are engaged.

> Take the shoulder blades toward one another and slide them down your back.

> Pressing your feet into the floor, inhale sweep your arms up, reaching to the sky.

> Exhale to forward fold, keeping a slight bend in the knees.

> *Experienced practitioner:* Inhale, lift your head and chest, step your right foot back, bring your right knee down, and take your arms up for low lunge (all on the inhale).

> *Beginner practitioner:* Inhale, lift your head and chest. Exhale, step your right foot back and bring your left knee to the ground. Inhale, lift your arms overhead. Take another full breath in low lunge if you need to before moving into the next pose (two to three breath cycles total).

> Exhale, bring your arms to the ground and step your left foot back, coming into plank. Lower yourself to the floor with knees, chest, and chin touching the mat.

> Inhale, engage the hands as if you're dragging yourself forward, and bring your chest forward and up into cobra or up dog.

> Exhale, curl your toes under, and press your hips up and back into down dog.

> If you feel that you need to stay in down dog for a few breaths, that's okay. Listen to your body.

> *Experienced practitioner:* Inhale, step your right foot forward, take your left knee down, and lift your arms up into low lunge (all in one inhalation).

> *Beginner practitioner:* Inhale, step your right foot forward. Exhale, bring your left knee down. Inhale, lift your arms up for low lunge.

> Exhale, step your left foot forward, coming into forward fold.

> If you feel that your body will benefit from staying longer in forward fold, then listen to your body and stay here for a few more breaths, shaking the head "yes" and "no" to release the neck.

> Inhale your arms up overhead, reaching for the sky.

> Exhale your arms down for mountain pose. Reengage the alignment principles if desired.

> Repeat up to twelve rounds of sun salutations according to your capacity and intention.

LOW BACK, HIPS, AND LEGS

YOU LEARNED IN THE ANATOMY CHAPTER that the muscles are connected to one another by a layer of connective tissue, and that tendons attach muscles to bones. The muscles, bones, and tendons of the low back, hip, and leg area are intimately connected to one another. Back pain is most often caused by chronically contracted hip flexors, and IT band pain can be the result of sleepy glutes. This means that stretching the low back by practicing a forward fold may actually exacerbate low back pain. Practicing an outer hip stretch for the IT band that also stretches the glutes can be counterproductive as well.

That chapter also emphasized the importance of strengthening the muscles we underuse in paddling and stretching the muscles that we overuse. Our hips, low backs, and legs experience a double whammy in our culture due to the time we spend sitting—at our desks, in our cars, watching TV, and so on. All that sitting can lead to chronically contracted hip flexors and hamstrings. Kayakers and canoeists also then sit in their boats. SUP paddlers are a little better off, but their lower bodies are still susceptible to imbalances. This chapter includes the poses for the low back, hips, and legs that, in my experience, have the greatest benefits for paddlers. Remember that the alignment principles are included in the cues for each pose, and you can choose to engage them or leave them out.

Opposite: Dancer pose at Looking Glass Falls, Pisgah National Forest, North Carolina

CAT/COW

This pose moves the spine through the motions of flexion and extension to cultivate and maintain suppleness, range of motion, and disk alignment. These movements also take the pelvis through anterior and posterior tilt positions. This helps
to move the hips through their full range of motion front to back and brings
balance to the muscles that surround the pelvis.

> Come to hands and knees on the mat, placing your hands mindfully
underneath your shoulders. Spread your fingers. Press the fingertip pads and
the balls of the index fingers into the mat, taking the weight out of the heels of
your hands.

> On an inhale, soften between the shoulder blades, take the sitz bones back and apart, move the tailbone toward the sky, and gaze up.

> On an exhale, press the hands into the floor to round the spine, then tuck the chin and round the low back.

> Repeat the motion five to ten times, synching the movement with the breath.

CHILD'S POSE

This pose allows the low back to lengthen and releases the mid and upper back, shoulders, and neck. It also lengthens the quads and the shins.

I've included child's pose because it's a very relaxing pose that's useful for transitions between poses or just taking a break. It's a great pose for stretching the low back without putting too much strain on the pelvis, and it feels really good. The modification I'm making for paddlers is to keep the arms extended forward to keep the shoulders from rolling forward.

> Come to hands and knees on the mat, and press the hips back toward the heels.

> Keep the hands forward and bring the forehead toward the floor. For paddlers it's especially important to practice child's pose with the arms forward, as it keeps the shoulders from rounding.

> For deeper relaxation inhale through the nose and let out an open-mouth sigh, relieving tension and stress. Do this up to three times.

> Hold for five deep and easy breaths in and out through the nose.

> This pose can be done with the knees together or apart. Knees apart allows room for your belly between your knees. Try both versions and see which is most comfortable for you. You may decide to practice both. For SUP paddlers who experience tired feet while paddling, practicing child's pose with the toes curled under is a great stretch.

DOWN DOG

Down dog is one of the most practiced poses in yoga. It helps to strengthen our paddling muscles in the upper back and shoulders, while allowing the neck and spine to release. The pose stretches the hamstrings, glutes, and calves and subtly releases muscles in the front of the hips and in the quadriceps. Down dog is also considered a gentle inversion.

> Start on your hands and knees, placing your hands mindfully underneath your shoulders. Spread your fingers. Press the fingertip pads and the balls of the index fingers into the mat, taking the weight out of the heels of your hands.

> Curl your toes under and press your hands into the mat to lift your hips up toward the sky.

> Keep a slight bend in the knees and press into your hands to take your sitz bones back and apart. Keeping this . . .

> Take your front low ribs down, expand your back ribs, and lengthen through the upper spine.

> Draw the shoulder blades back and down.

> Release the head and neck, allowing them to lengthen from the spine.

> You can add movement by bending one knee and then the other, or lifting one hip and then the other.

> Come back to center and hold the pose for five deep and easy breaths.

> After a few breaths, gently invite your heels toward the floor while keeping a soft bend in the knees and the sitz bones moving back and apart.

LOW LUNGE

Low lunge lengthens the hip flexors and quadriceps, both chronically contracted muscles in paddlers. This pose also strengthens the glutes in the front leg when the heel of the front foot is pressing into the floor.

BASIC POSE

> There are a few different ways to move into this pose. The first is to start on your hands and knees and step one foot forward between your hands. The other is to start in down dog (see above) and step your foot forward between your hands. Another is to start from standing, step one leg back, and take your back knee down. It doesn't matter which transition you use. Explore, and find what transition works best for your body. I'm going to start us in down dog.

> From down dog, step your left foot forward between your hands.

> Take your back knee down, while keeping your hands on either side of your front foot.

> If necessary, move your front foot forward until your front knee is in line with your front ankle, with your front knee bent at a 90-degree angle. Keep your back toes curled under for support and as a gentle stretch to the foot. Keep your hands on either side of the front foot.

> Press the front heel into the mat to engage the back of the front leg, and take the sitz bones back and apart. This will lift your hips slightly away from the floor and change the feel of the stretch.

> Keeping the above alignment, press your back knee into the floor and lengthen up through your hip flexor.

> Hold for five deep and easy breaths.

> Switch sides and repeat.

LOW LUNGE WITH HANDS ON THIGH

> Starting in the variation of low lunge described above, press down through the front heel and the back knee to lift your torso up. Place your hands on your front thigh.

> Take the sitz bones back and apart while you continue to press down through the front heel and back knee.

> Take your front low ribs down, expand your back ribs, and lengthen through the upper spine and out the crown of the head.

> Draw the shoulder blades back and down.

> Keep checking back through all the alignment pieces as you hold the pose for five deep and easy breaths.

> Switch sides and repeat.

LOW LUNGE WITH ARMS EXTENDED

> From the hands-on-thigh variation of low lunge, press the front heel and back knee into the mat to lengthen through the torso, then lift the arms up overhead.

> Retake the sitz bones back and apart.

> Take your front low ribs down, expand your back ribs, and lengthen through the upper spine and out the crown of the head.

> Draw the shoulder blades back and down.

> Gaze upward for a subtle back bend.

> Hold for five deep and easy breaths.

> Switch sides and repeat.

RUNNER'S STRETCH (HALF SPLIT)

This pose lengthens the hamstring and calf muscles of the front leg.

> From a hands-and-knees position, step one foot forward between your hands, or start in low lunge.

> Shift your hips back to lengthen through the front leg.

> Flex your front foot and spread your toes, keeping your front heel on the ground.

> Keep a slight bend in the front knee and take the sitz bones back and apart, lengthening through the hamstring of the front leg.

> Press the heel of the front foot deeper into the mat.

> Keep length through your spine and a lift in the chest.

> Hold for five deep and easy breaths.

> Switch sides and repeat.

> If you want to also explore a stretch in your IT band (outside of the leg), try turning your front toes out to the side.

THIGH STRETCH ON BELLY

This pose lengthens the quadriceps and releases the hip flexor muscles in the front of the hips. It also lengthens through the pectorals and shoulder while engaging the upper back.

> Lie on your belly.

> Prop yourself up on your left forearm with the forearm placed parallel to the front of the mat.

> Press into your left forearm to reach back and take your right ankle or foot with your right hand.

> Gently press both knees into the floor to take the sitz bones back and apart (the hip creases will lift away from the floor slightly) while pressing the right foot down toward your right hip.

> Stretch from the right hip through the right knee while keeping the sitz bones back and apart.

> Take your front low ribs down, expand your back ribs, and lengthen through the upper spine.

> Draw the right shoulder blade back and down.

> Gently invite your right rib cage to twist toward the floor.

> Hold for five deep and easy breaths.

> Switch sides and repeat.

WINDSHIELD WIPER POSE

This is one of my favorite poses for paddlers, and I practice it often. It's a passive, deep, and relaxing stretch for the hip flexors.

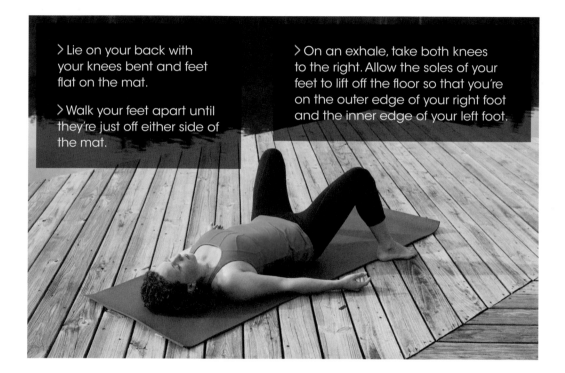

> Lie on your back with your knees bent and feet flat on the mat.

> Walk your feet apart until they're just off either side of the mat.

> On an exhale, take both knees to the right. Allow the soles of your feet to lift off the floor so that you're on the outer edge of your right foot and the inner edge of your left foot.

I actually love to bring movement to this pose before I settle into it. I start with my feet wider than the mat distance apart and knees bent. Then I exhale both knees to the right, inhale them back to center, and exhale both knees to the left. This movement from side to side is where the name "windshield wiper pose" comes from.

> If you want to feel a deeper stretch in your left hip flexor, walk your left foot farther to the left.

> Take your left arm, or both arms, overhead and outstretched on the floor. If this isn't available to you, then extend your arms out to the sides. The key is to find an arm position that feels relaxing.

> Relax and allow your body to sink into the floor.

> Use the three-count belly breath technique from chapter 4, and see if you can start the breath in the left hip. Breathe into the left hip as if you could actually send air there.

> If you feel any pain or discomfort in your left knee, first flex your left foot and spread your left toes to see if it dissipates. If not, then back out of the pose or hold it for less time.

> Hold for five deep and easy breaths.

> Switch sides and repeat.

BRIDGE POSE

Bridge pose strengthens the glutes and opens the chest and shoulders while strengthening the upper back, making it an awesome pose for paddlers.

> Lie on your back with your knees bent and feet flat on the floor, sitz bones distance apart. Check that your toes are pointed straight ahead so that your feet are parallel to each other.

> Walk your feet back toward your hips until your heels are in line with the bend of your knees.

> Press your feet, especially your heels and big toes, into the floor to lift your hips off the floor.

> Walk your shoulder blades underneath you to lift and open the chest.

> You can keep your elbows pressing into the floor with your fingertips toward the sky (see photo), or you can clasp your hands under your back and walk your shoulder blades under even more.

> Press the back of the head gently into the mat and lift the chin slightly to maintain the natural curve of the cervical spine.

> Imagine that your knees are gently holding a block between them so that they are engaged and don't splay out.

> Take the sitz bones back and apart, softening the creases of the hips. This action will lower your hips toward the floor slightly. Keep this and . . .

> Engage the feet as if you were dragging them up toward your shoulders.

> Hold for five deep and easy breaths.

> Release your hands and lower your hips to come out of the pose.

> Notice the sensations in your body and mind.

ONE-LEGGED BRIDGE

This pose targets and strengthens the glutes.

> Lie on your back with your knees bent and feet flat on the floor about sitz bones distance apart. Check that your toes are pointed straight ahead and feet are parallel.

> Walk your feet toward your hips until your heels are underneath your knees.

> Extend your right leg up toward the sky with the heel pressing up and the toes spread.

> Inhale to press your left foot, especially the heel and big toe, into the floor to lift your hips up.

> Exhale and lower your hips back down to the floor.

> Repeat ten times on each side, combining movement and breath.

RECLINED HAND TO BIG TOE POSE

This pose may be one of the most beneficial poses for paddlers. It stretches all sides of the hips and the hamstrings while keeping the spine in alignment. The back positioned against the floor keeps the pelvis from having too much posterior tilt. In fact, lying on the back in this pose makes it easier to engage and feel the benefits of some of the alignment principles. This is one of my go-to poses on a daily basis.

This pose requires a strap.

> Lie on your back with your knees bent, feet flat on the mat, and your strap within reach.

> Take your strap, lift your right leg, and place the strap around the ball of your right foot, letting equal amounts of strap drape from either side of the foot.

> Cross the strap to make an X in front of your shin, and hold one end in each hand.

> Extend the right leg up toward the sky, keeping a soft bend in the knee while extending your left leg onto the floor with your left toes toward the sky.

> Hold the straps close to your chest, not close to your foot. This variation of the pose isn't about pulling the extended leg toward your chest. Holding the ends of the straps close to your chest allows you to draw your shoulder blades together and create lift in your chest. For paddlers, creating lift in the chest is more important than drawing the leg toward the chest.

> Press the ball of the foot firmly into the strap and spread the toes.

> *Do not* try to hold your extended leg at a 90-degree angle to your body unless you can do so *and* still take the sitz bones back and apart at the same time. Let the leg drop slightly toward the floor until you feel that you can effectively take the sitz bones back and apart. You can also think of pressing your tailbone into the floor, creating anterior tilt in your pelvis (having a curve in your lumbar spine).

> Take your front low ribs down, expand your back ribs, and lengthen through the upper spine. You will feel a subtle stretch in the low back.

> Hold for five deep and easy breaths.

> Take both ends of the strap and hold them in your right hand.

> Keeping your sitz bones moving back and apart, slowly take your right leg out to the right without pulling it toward you. Go only as far as you can without your left hip lifting off the floor. The goal is to feel a stretch across the front of your left hip. If you're pulling your right leg too far toward your upper body, it creates a lot of posterior tilt in the pelvis and doesn't allow for length in the left hip flexor.

> Take your front low ribs down, expand your back ribs, and lengthen through the upper spine.

> Hold for five deep and easy breaths.

> Bring the leg back to center on an inhale.

> Cross your straps again, creating an X in front of your shin and holding one end in each hand.

> Take the right leg across the midline about 10 degrees to the left without pulling it toward you.

> Take the sitz bones back and apart.

> Take your front low ribs down, expand your back ribs, and lengthen through the upper spine.

> Hold for five deep and easy breaths. This part of the pose lengthens the IT band and also gets into the quadratus lumborum.

> Finally, hold both ends of the strap in your left hand and take the right leg all the way across the body toward the floor. Keep holding on to the strap and extend your leg in this reclined twist, or release the strap and let the leg relax in the twist.

> Hold for five deep and easy breaths.

> To finish, bring the leg back to center and extend it, maintaining a soft knee before releasing the strap and allowing the leg to float down.

> Pause, lying on the floor for a few breaths. Notice the difference between both hips and legs before moving on to the other side.

HIGH LUNGE

This pose strengthens the front leg while lengthening the hip flexors of the back leg. When the arms are lifted overhead, there is activation of the upper back muscles and an opening in the chest.

> Standing at the front of your mat, step your left leg back about one leg length.

> Keep your back heel lifted and your back knee bent. Your front knee is bent directly over your front ankle.

> Lower your torso until you can place your hands on the mat on either side of your front foot.

FIRST VARIATION

> Keep your hands on either side of your front foot.

> Press into the floor with the heel and big toe of your front foot, as well as the toes of your back foot.

> Take the sitz bones back and apart.

> Take your front low ribs down, expand your back ribs, and lengthen through the upper spine.

SECOND VARIATION

> Press into the floor with the heel and big toe of your front foot and the toes of your back foot.

> Inhale, rise up, and take your hands to your hips.

> Take the sitz bones back and apart.

> Take your front low ribs down, expand your back ribs, and lengthen through the upper spine.

THIRD VARIATION

> Press into the floor with the heel and big toe of your front foot and the toes of your back foot.

> Inhale, rise up, and lift your arms overhead.

> Take the sitz bones back and apart.

> Take your front low ribs down, expand your back ribs, and lengthen through the upper spine.

> Gaze up, initiating a gentle back bend.

> Hold for five deep and easy breaths.

> Switch sides and repeat.

LOW LUNGE HOLDING BACK FOOT

The next two variations of low lunge provide a deeper stretch for the hip flexors and quads of the back leg and for the chest and shoulders. They also strengthen the upper back.

WITH ONE HAND

> Come into low lunge with your right foot forward and your hands on either side of your front foot.

> Walk your left hand out to the side until it's off the mat.

> Weight the left arm, bend your left knee, and reach back with your right hand to take hold of your left foot.

> Take the sitz bones back and apart. This will lift the hips away from the floor.

> Take your front low ribs down, expand your back ribs, and lengthen through the upper spine.

> Take your right shoulder blade back and down and open your chest to the sky, lengthening through the crown of the head.

> Hold for five deep and easy breaths.

> Switch sides and repeat.

WITH BOTH HANDS

> Come into low lunge with your right foot forward and your hands on either side of your front foot.

> Rise up and place your hands on your front thigh.

> Bend your left knee and reach back with your left hand to take hold of your back foot.

> Take the sitz bones back and apart, and lengthen through the crown of the head.

> Options are to lift your right arm to the sky or keep it on your thigh.

> Take your front low ribs down, expand your back ribs, and lengthen through the upper spine.

> Press your back knee strongly into the mat as you lengthen out the crown of the head.

> To take the pose deeper, reach back with your right hand, and hold your foot with both hands.

> Retake the sitz bones back and apart.

> Retake your front low ribs down, expand your back ribs, and lengthen through the upper spine and out the crown of the head.

> Hold for five deep and easy breaths.

> Switch sides and repeat.

TRIANGLE POSE

Triangle pose is a standing hip opener with a twist that stretches and strengthens the legs, side body, torso, and back. It provides a nice opening across the chest and shoulders.

> Stand at the front of your mat with your feet sitz bones distance apart and parallel.

> Step your left leg back one leg length.

> Lower your back heel down and turn your back toes out so that the sole of your back foot is flat on the mat. Look back to check that the outer edge of your back foot is in line with the outer edge of the mat.

> Inhale your arms up until they are extended out at shoulder height.

> Bend slightly in both knees, and take the sitz bones back and apart.

> Press strongly into the mat with the outer edge of your back foot.

> Inhale, take your front low ribs down, expand your back ribs, and lengthen through the upper spine.

> Exhale, using the power of your feet pressing strongly into the mat, take your right hand down to your right thigh and extend your left arm up toward the sky.

> Bring awareness once again to your alignment principles.

> Hold for five deep and easy breaths.

> To take the pose deeper, slowly slide your front hand down to your shin, ankle, or to the inside or outside of your front foot. Where you place your hand depends on your body's capacity. Only slide your hand down as far as you can without hinging forward from the waist. Your body should be aligned as if it were sandwiched between two panes of glass. Listen to your body and find the position that feels both easeful and steady.

> To come out of the pose, press into your back foot as you inhale up, or take your top hand down to the floor and step back into down dog.

> Switch sides and repeat.

WARRIOR II

This pose activates the legs while opening the hips. Muscles that activate in this pose are the glutes and TFL of the back hip/leg and the hamstrings and glutes of the front leg. The TFL and psoas of the back leg lengthen. There is extension through the chest, biceps, and forearms, as well as engagement of the upper back. Warrior II is a pose that inspires strength, stamina, courage, and confidence.

> Stand at the front of your mat with your feet sitz bones distance apart and parallel.

> Step your left leg back one leg length.

> Lower your back heel down so that the outer edge of your back foot is in line with the outer edge of the mat.

> Inhale your arms up until they are extended out at shoulder height.

> Bend your front knee, keeping it stacked over your front ankle.

> Bend slightly in your back knee, and take the sitz bones back and apart.

> Press strongly into the mat with the outer edge of your back foot.

> Inhale, take your front low ribs down, expand your back ribs, and lengthen through the upper spine and out the crown of the head.

> Gaze past the fingers of your front hand.

> Hold for five deep and easy breaths.

> Step forward to release the pose.

> Switch sides and repeat.

WIDE LEGGED FORWARD FOLD

The wide stance of this hamstring stretch is more suitable for paddlers than a regular standing forward fold with the feet closer together because it allows more room for the pelvis to tilt anteriorly (water pouring out onto the floor in front of you), which helps to protect the low back and spine. In my experience, kayakers and canoeists tend to experience low back pain and disk herniations from long hours of sitting in their boats. Performing a regular forward fold where the low back is rounded (posteriorly tilted) can exacerbate low back discomfort and injury. Wide legged forward fold also makes it easier to take the sitz bones back and apart to give length to the hamstrings, while also allowing the hip flexors to soften. If you can't reach the floor between your feet in this pose, then place blocks underneath your hands. This pose is considered a gentle inversion.

> Start standing with your legs one leg length apart, facing the side of your mat with your toes facing straight ahead and parallel. You can look to see that the outer edges of your feet are parallel with the outer edges of your mat.

> Place your hands on your hips, take a slight bend in the knees, and inhale, lengthening through the crown of the head.

> Exhale, fold forward at the waist, and bring your hands to the floor between your feet or to blocks that you've placed on the floor in front of you.

> Keep the slight bend in the knees and take the sitz bones back and apart while pressing your feet into the floor.

> Shift your weight into your heels while keeping the balls of the feet pressing down into the floor.

> Inhale. Lift the head and the chest. It should feel as if you're stretching your upper body forward while stretching your sitz bones back.

> Exhale to fold forward again.

> Draw your shoulder blades back and down (away from your ears), and let your neck extend and your head hang from the spine. Shake your head "yes" and "no," and take an open-mouth sigh to release any tension.

> Hold for five deep and easy breaths.

> To come out of the pose, place your hands on your hips, inhale to press your feet into the floor, and rise all the way up.

CHAIR POSE/SQUAT

Chair pose is a key pose for waking up sleepy glutes and strengthening both the backs and fronts of the legs. It also strengthens the core.

> Stand at the front of your mat with your feet sitz bones distance apart and parallel.

> Shift your center of mass into your heels, and feel the backs of the legs activate.

> Inhale to press through the heels and the big toes, bending the knees and shifting your hips back while taking your arms up overhead.

> Look down to see that your knees are stacked more over the front of your ankles and not forward of your feet. This will bring more activation to the backs of the legs and glutes.

> Hold for five deep and easy breaths.

> Stand up to release the pose.

> For extra glute strengthening, repeat this pose two or three times.

STANDING THIGH STRETCH

This is one of the easiest and most beneficial poses for kayakers to do right after they get out of their kayaks. It activates the muscles in the standing leg and lengthens the hip flexors and quads of the bent leg. The upper back gets activated, and the chest and fronts of the shoulders lengthen. The core engages to stabilize as the body balances on one foot.

> Stand at the front of your mat with your feet sitz bones distance apart and parallel.

> Inhale to bend your left knee, and reach back to take your left ankle or foot with your left hand.

> If you need support for balance, use a wall, chair, bench, or friend!

> Keep your knees close to each other.

> Keep a slight bend in the standing knee, and take the sitz bones back and apart.

> Inhale, take your front low ribs down, expand your back ribs, and lengthen through the upper spine and out the crown of the head.

> Press your foot strongly into your hand.

> Think about lengthening from your hip down and out your bent knee, and from your hip up and out the crown of your head.

> Hold for five deep and easy breaths.

> Switch sides and repeat.

DANCER POSE PREP

This pose takes standing thigh stretch one step further. It provides more lengthening of the hip flexors and quads of the bent leg, as well as the chest and shoulders. It is also a more challenging balance pose that works on strengthening the standing leg and requires stronger core activation.

> Come into standing thigh stretch with your left hand holding your left ankle or foot.

> Externally rotate your left shoulder to hold the inside edge of your left foot with your thumb on the ball of the foot and your fingers on the top of the foot.

> Shift your center of mass back into your right heel.

> Take the sitz bones back and apart.

> Inhale, take your front low ribs down, expand your back ribs, and lengthen through the upper spine and out the crown of the head.

> Extend your right arm up.

> Press your left foot into your hand to lift your hand back and up, while gently pressing your back hand against your foot for resistance.

> Use the power of your foot pressing into your hand to hinge forward at the waist.

> Press the right foot, especially the heel, into the floor strongly, and continue to extend out the crown of the head.

> Hold for five deep and easy breaths.

> To come out of the pose, unhinge your body, lengthening through the crown of the head, and then release your back foot to the floor.

> Switch sides and repeat.

SIDE BODY

THE MUSCLES OF THE SIDE BODY are mainly responsible for lateral flexion of the spine and hiking the hip. Kayakers and canoeists activate these muscles for hip snaps, performing the roll, edge control, and stability. SUP paddlers also use these muscles for balance and stability on the board, and when carrying the board by the handle. Stretching and strengthening the side body for full range of motion helps paddlers achieve better balance and control when paddling.

*Opposite: Getting bendy on
Lake Jocassee, South Carolina.*

SIDE STRETCH VARIATION

This pose lengthens the top side body while activating the bottom side body. It also strengthens the core.

> Start on hands and knees in the middle of your mat.

> Keeping your left knee on the mat, take your right foot out to the right, as if it were a kickstand on a bike.

> Extend the right foot back and place the right heel down so that the outer edge of the back (right) foot is in line with the outer edge of the mat. Keep the right knee slightly bent, and press the outer edge of the right foot strongly into the ground.

> Take your left shoulder blade back and down, and extend your right arm up to the sky.

> Take the sitz bones back and apart.

> Take your front low ribs down, expand your back ribs, and lengthen through the upper spine and out the crown of the head.

> Take five deep and easy breaths.

> Extend your right arm over your right ear, palm facing down.

> Stretch from the outer edge of your back foot through the right fingertips. For more of a challenge, turn your chest open toward the sky to add a small twist and chest opener to the pose.

> Take five deep and easy breaths.

> Switch sides and repeat.

GATE POSE

This side stretch lengthens the side body, hip flexors, and glutes of the top side of the body. It also lengthens the hamstrings of the extended leg. Activation happens in the glutes and obliques of the bottom side of the body.

> Start on your knees with your toes curled under while facing the long side of the mat.

> Extend your left leg out to the left, and place the sole of your foot flat on the mat with toes pointing forward.

> Press your right knee into the ground strongly as you extend your right arm up on an inhale.

> Exhale to hinge over to the left, sliding your left hand down your left leg until you reach your edge of steadiness and ease.

> Keep a slight bend in the extended leg.

> Take the sitz bones back and apart.

> Take your front low ribs down, expand your back ribs, and lengthen through the upper spine and out the crown of the head.

> Take five deep and easy breaths.

> Switch sides and repeat.

SIDE-PLANK VARIATION WITH SIDE STRETCH

This is another of my favorite yoga shapes because it feels so good. It lengthens the obliques and the quadratus lumborum of the bottom side body while softening the hip flexors.

> Lie on your right side with your right leg extended. Bend your left knee and place your left foot flat on the mat with toes facing forward in front of the right leg. Be sure that you're exactly on your side, not leaning back or forward.

> Prop yourself up on your right forearm.

> Press the floor away with your right elbow and forearm.

> Press your right hip down into the floor and extend out the sole of your right foot.

> Take the sitz bones back and apart.

> Inhale, take your front low ribs down, expand your back ribs, and lengthen through the upper spine and out the crown of the head.

> Your left forearm rests on your left knee.

> If you want a deeper stretch, extend your right arm (come up onto your hand) and take your right shoulder blade back and down.

> Hold for five deep and easy breaths.

> Switch sides and repeat.

PALM TREE

Palm tree is another great side opener that lengthens the top side body. It also promotes deeper lateral flexion of the spine.

> Stand at the front of your mat with your feet sitz bones distance apart and parallel.

> Inhale your arms up toward the sky and place the palms together with the index fingers high.

> Exhale.

> Inhale and press your right foot into the ground. Keep a soft bend in the knees and lengthen your right side up toward the sky.

> Exhale and hinge over to the left while your right foot continues to press into the ground.

> Take the sitz bones back and apart.

> Inhale, take your front low ribs down, expand your back ribs, and lengthen through the upper spine and out the crown of the head.

> Hold for five deep and easy breaths, breathing into your right side as if you could send air there.

> Inhale to come back to center, and exhale to release the pose.

> Switch sides and repeat.

SIDE ANGLE STRETCH

In addition to stretching the top side body, this pose is a hip opener that also strengthens the legs.

> Start standing at the front of your mat with your feet sitz bones distance apart and parallel.

> Step your right foot back one leg length.

> Lower your back heel down so that the outer edge of your back foot is in line with the outer edge of the mat.

> Keep a slight bend in the back knee and deeply bend the front knee, keeping it in line with the front ankle.

> Take the sitz bones back and apart, and press the heels into the floor to bring tone to the back of the legs.

> Press the back foot strongly into the mat, to take your front forearm to your front thigh, and extend your back arm by your top ear.

> Enjoy the side stretch from the outer edge of your back foot pressing down all the way through your top fingertips stretching forward.

> Hold for five deep and easy breaths.

> To add a slight twist and chest opener, press your forearm into your front thigh to turn your chest toward the sky, and gently take the shoulder blades back and down.

> Inhale to lift out of the pose, or exhale to take your top arm down and step back into down dog.

> Switch sides and repeat.

> Start in triangle pose (see chapter 7) or side angle stretch with forearm on thigh.

> Keep coming back to the alignment principles while you hold the pose.

HALF MOON

This is a more vigorous standing side body lengthener that also activates core and balance.

> Start in triangle pose (see chapter 7).

> Bend the front knee and place your front hand to the outside and in front of your front foot.

> Lift your back foot off the ground and raise the leg up to hip height with the back foot flexed so that the bottom of your foot is flat, as if it were standing on the floor.

> Take the sitz bones back and apart.

> Take your front low ribs down, expand your back ribs, and lengthen through the upper spine and out the crown of the head.

> Extend from the back foot through the crown of the head.

> Keep your gaze down to the floor, or turn your head and gaze up toward your top arm.

> Hold for five deep and easy breaths, and don't be afraid to fall!

> Lower your back foot to its starting position and move through triangle before coming out of the pose.

> Switch sides and repeat.

SIDE PLANK

The top side body in side plank experiences lengthening, while the bottom side body strengthens and stabilizes. This is also a core strengthener.

> Come to hands and knees on the mat, placing your hands mindfully underneath your shoulders. Spread your fingers. Press the fingertip pads and the balls of the index fingers into the mat, taking the weight out of the heels of your hands.

> If you want more of a challenge, try activating the alignment principles in this pose.

> Lift your knees off the floor and come up onto your toes.

> Turn onto the outside edge of your left foot and stack your right foot on top of the left.

> Extend your right arm up toward the sky.

> Lift your hips away from the floor.

> Gaze forward or turn your head to gaze up toward the top arm.

> Hold for five deep and easy breaths.

> Switch sides and repeat.

NECK, SHOULDERS, AND UPPER BACK

ALL PADDLERS, REGARDLESS OF THEIR CRAFT, tend to experience chronically contracted pectorals and sleepy upper backs. This combination can increase the risk for shoulder discomfort, weakness, and injury. It's important for paddlers to lengthen the pectorals and strengthen the muscles of the upper back so that the shoulders can return to optimal alignment. The trigger points that paddlers often feel in their shoulder blades do not need to be stretched, they actually need to be strengthened. Their root cause is weak upper back muscles working really hard to counteract the forward pull of the pectorals. When the upper back muscles are strengthened, they don't have to work so hard because there is more balance between the front and back of the body. This balance helps to protect the shoulders from risk of injury. The neck can also become tight and sore due to the paddling motion and carrying our boats and boards. As I mentioned in chapter 3, the alignment cue to take the front low ribs down, expand the back ribs, and lengthen through the spine out the crown of the head may make it feel as though you can't go as deep into backbends as you're accustomed to. That's okay and good for the alignment of your rib cage. It creates more space in the torso and low back compared with jutting the ribs forward, which can lead to the crunching of the low back. I invite you to try it to see how it feels for you.

Opposite: Wild Thing at Triple Falls in Dupont State Forest, North Carolina.

SIMPLE BACK BEND

This is a very gentle back bend available to all levels of practitioner. It opens the chest, strengthens the upper back, and extends the spine.

> Sit cross-legged on a few blankets placed on your mat. This will help you to sit comfortably for several minutes.

> Reach back and move the flesh out from under your sitz bones so that you can sit up taller.

> Take your hands behind your hips, up on your fingertips.

> Inhale to press the sitz bones down, and press your hands into the floor.

> Take the front low ribs down, expand through the back ribs, and extend up through the upper spine. This alignment principle is especially important when practicing back bends to keep the front ribs from jutting forward and crunching the low back. Take your shoulder blades toward each other, and lift your collarbone toward the sky.

> Lift the chin slightly to maintain the natural curve in the cervical spine.

> Hold for five deep and easy breaths.

SIMPLE NECK STRETCH

This gentle neck stretch lengthens the muscles in the neck and helps to relieve tension.

> Sit cross-legged on your mat. Place a few blankets on the mat if needed, for ease of sitting for several minutes.

> Reach back and move the flesh out from under your sitz bones so that you can sit up taller.

> Inhale the arms up until they are at a diagonal from the neck and pointed toward the floor.

> Extend from the shoulders through the fingertips.

> Inhale, extend through the crown of the head.

> Exhale, draw your right ear toward your right shoulder while continuing to stretch through the fingertips.

> Pause and hold for five deep, slow breaths. Breathe into your neck as if you could actually send air there.

> Inhale to bring your head back to center.

> Exhale the left ear to the left shoulder, and extend through the fingertips.

> Add movement to this pose by lifting the chin up toward the sky, or turning the chin down toward the chest to stretch different sides of the neck.

SPIDER COBRA

This is a therapeutic version of cobra pose that works to strengthen the upper back while broadening the chest and shoulders. The positioning of the arms and hands in this pose makes it easy to draw the shoulder blades back and down, strengthening the upper back.

> Lie on your belly with your forehead on the floor.

> Extend your arms out from your shoulders with your elbows bent at 90-degree angles and pointed toward the sky.

> Bring your hands up on your fingertips.

> Bend your knees slightly and gently press them into the floor to draw the sitz bones back and apart.

> Lengthen from your hips and out through your toes.

> Press your fingers into the floor, especially your thumbs, to squeeze your shoulder blades toward each other.

> Take your front low ribs down, expand the back ribs, and extend through the spine and out the crown of the head. Notice how this alignment principle changes the feel of the pose.

> Hold for five deep and easy breaths.

> You can also bring movement to this pose by taking the left ear toward the left shoulder and then the right ear toward the right shoulder to add a neck stretch.

SECOND VARIATION

> In spider cobra, press your fingertips, and especially your thumbs, into the floor as if you were going to drag yourself forward on the mat.

> Using the pressure of your fingertips into the floor, draw your chest slightly forward and up without losing the squeeze of the shoulder blades.

> Take your front low ribs down, expand the back ribs, and extend through the spine and out the crown of the head. Notice how this alignment principle changes the feel of the pose. You're expanding through both the front and the back ribs.

> Hold for five deep and easy breaths.

COBRA

> Lie on your belly with your gaze to the floor.

> Place your hands, palms flat, beside and in line with the middle of your chest.

> Bend your knees slightly and gently press them into the floor to draw the sitz bones back and apart.

> Lengthen from your hips and out through your toes.

> Press your hands into the floor as if you were going to drag yourself forward.

> Draw the chest slightly forward and up, drawing the shoulders back and squeezing the shoulder blades toward each other.

> Take your front low ribs down, expand the back ribs, and extend through the spine and out the crown of the head. Notice how this alignment principle changes the feel of the pose.

> Hold for five deep and easy breaths.

SUPPORTED CHEST OPENER WITH BLOCKS

This pose is very relaxing and allows for a deep, passive opening through the chest and shoulders. It's a wonderful restorative pose for paddlers.

> Place two yoga blocks together in a line with the longer and thinner side up.

> Sit about a foot in front of the blocks with your knees bent and feet flat on the mat.

> Lie back on the blocks so that the edge of the block closest to you supports the middle of your back. If you were to draw an imaginary line from the point on your back where the edge of the block sits, through your body to your chest, it would hit in the middle of your chest. Your head is supported by the second block.

> Keep your knees bent and feet flat on the mat.

> Take your arms out to the sides with your elbows bent at a 90-degree angle and your palms facing up toward the ceiling.

> Bring movement to this shape by drawing your elbows down toward the sides of your body and then extending them up by your ears. The movement is similar to a bird drying its wings in the sun.

> As you move, notice any spots that feel really good, and pause there for a few breaths.

> While you pause, take the sitz bones back and apart.

> Take your front low ribs down, expand the back ribs into the block, and extend through the spine and out the crown of the head.

> Continue to move and hold for as long as feels good.

> To come out of the pose, roll off the blocks to one side and press yourself up to sitting.

MOUNTAIN POSE WITH HANDS BEHIND BACK

This is a standing chest opener that is easy to do right before and/or after paddling. It opens the pectorals and strengthens the upper back.

> Stand in mountain pose with your feet parallel and sitz bones distance apart.

> Inhale your arms up toward the sky, then exhale to take your arms down and back, clasping your hands behind your back at your sacrum.

> Keep your elbows bent and squeeze them toward each other, pressing the shoulder blades toward each other.

> Take the sitz bones back and apart.

> Inhale, take your front low ribs down, expand the back ribs, and lengthen through the upper spine out the crown of the head.

> Exhale.

> Inhale, keep the shoulder blades and elbows pressing back, and lengthen your arms if it's available to you. If not, simply keep your arms bent and work the squeezing of the upper back, lifting the collarbone toward the sky and opening the chest.

> Hold for five full and mindful breaths.

SHOULDER BLADE PUSH-UPS

This is one of the best upper back strengtheners for paddlers. It moves the muscles that stabilize and move the shoulder blades through their full range of motion, including both lengthening and strengthening the serratus anterior. This is an effective pose for relieving trigger points in the shoulder blades, and is a go-to posture/exercise for me when my shoulders feel tweaked from paddling.

> Come to your knees and forearms with your hands clasped.

> Walk your knees back a few inches so that you are in a forearm plank position on your knees.

> Keep your sitz bones moving back and apart, draw your front low ribs down, and expand through the back ribs. Notice the core engagement that happens as a result of these alignment principles.

> Inhale and squeeze your shoulder blades toward each other.

> Exhale and pull your shoulder blades away from each other, rounding your upper back.

> It's important to isolate the movement to your shoulder blades. Your hips should not be lowering and lifting, and your spine should not be flexing and extending. Keep your lower body steady. The benefits come from the movement of your shoulder blades, not from the rest of your body.

> Repeat five to ten times, combining movement with breath.

DOLPHIN POSE

Dolphin pose is a down dog variation and forearm balance prep. It actively strengthens the upper back, lengthens the pectorals, and engages the core. It's considered a gentle inversion.

> Come to your knees and forearms on your mat. Your hands can be clasped or your palms flat on the mat.

> Curl your toes under and press your hips up and back to come into a down dog on your forearms.

> Press your forearms into the mat to take your chest toward your feet.

> Bend your knees slightly, take the sitz bones back and apart, and lengthen through the spine.

> Take your shoulder blades toward one another and down the back away from your ears.

> Relax your head toward the floor.

> Hold for five deep and easy breaths.

> To release the pose, come back to forearms and knees.

BRIDGE POSE

I'm including bridge pose in both the hips and shoulders chapters because it targets both areas of the body and is an important prep pose for more advanced back bends such as wheel.

Bridge pose strengthens the glutes and opens the chest and shoulders while strengthening the upper back, making it an awesome pose for paddlers.

> Lie on your back with your knees bent and feet flat on the floor and sitz bones distance apart. Check that your toes are pointed straight ahead so that your feet are parallel.

> Walk your feet back toward your hips until your heels are in line with the bend of your knees.

> Press your feet, especially the heels and big toes, into the floor to lift your hips off the floor.

> Walk your shoulder blades underneath you to lift and open the chest.

> You can keep your elbows pressing into the floor with your fingertips toward the sky or you can clasp your hands together under your back and walk your shoulder blades under even more (see photo).

> Press the back of the head gently into the mat and lift the chin slightly to maintain the natural curve of the cervical spine.

> Imagine that your knees are gently holding a block between them so that they are engaged and don't splay out.

> Take the sitz bones back and apart, softening the creases of the hips. This action will lower your hips toward the floor slightly. Keep this and . . .

> Engage the feet as if you were dragging them up toward your shoulders.

> Hold for five deep and easy breaths.

> Release your hands and lower your hips to come out of the pose.

> Notice the sensations in your body and mind.

UPWARD BOW POSE

This is a hip, chest, and shoulder opener, and an upper back strengthener. A good pose to practice for preparation is thigh stretch on belly (see chapter 7).

Upward bow has many benefits for paddlers including lengthening the abdominals, hip flexors, quadriceps, and pectorals. It's essentially the opposite of sitting, so it is especially beneficial for kayakers and canoeists.

> Lie on your belly.

> Reach back with both hands and clasp your ankles.

> Press the knees gently toward the floor and take the sitz bones back and apart. Engaging this alignment principle in this pose may feel more challenging than in other poses.

> Keep this as you take your front low ribs down, expand through the back ribs, and lengthen through the upper spine and out the crown of the head. This alignment principle will definitely feel challenging, as most of us thrust the front ribs forward to get into this pose. Thrusting the front ribs forward here can lead to crunching in the low back. Engaging this alignment principle helps to protect the low back.

> On your next inhale press your feet into your hands to lift the chest and thighs away from the floor. Resist the temptation to let go of all the alignment principles.

> Keep your knees gently squeezing toward each other.

> Hold for five deep and easy breaths.

> Come back down to your belly to rest. Notice the sensations in your body and mind.

> Child's pose is a nice counter pose to practice after upward bow.

WHEEL

Wheel is an advanced and deep hip, chest, and shoulder opener that requires preparation and practice. I highly recommend that you practice and feel comfortable with bridge pose and upward bow before attempting this pose.

> Lie on your back with your knees bent and your feet flat on your mat.

> Walk your feet back toward your hips until your heels are underneath your knees.

> Be sure that your feet are parallel and toes are facing straight ahead.

> Take your elbows toward the sky and place your hands palms flat, fingers slightly turned out, on either side of your ears. Activate your hands like a tripod, distributing the weight evenly through the hand.

> Take your sitz bones back and apart, and draw your shoulder blades down and back. Keeping this . . .

> Inhale and press into your hands and feet to lift your hips up toward the sky. Keep pressing the feet into the floor to lengthen through your legs and hips, and press your chest forward toward your hands.

> Draw your shoulder blades toward each other to create a deeper chest opening.

> Once you're up in the pose, take your sitz bones back and apart. This will lower your hips slightly toward the ground.

> Take your front low ribs down, expand the back ribs, and lengthen through the upper spine. This will also feel like you are coming out of the chest opener slightly.

> Notice how these alignment principles feel in the pose.

> Breathe deeply and easily for up to five breaths.

> To come out of the pose, tuck your chin into your chest and lower slowly and gently.

> Notice the sensations in your body and mind.

> Hugging your knees into your chest and/or a reclined twist can be a nice counterpose.

CORE STRENGTHENERS

CORE STRENGTH IS AN IMPORTANT ELEMENT of effective paddling technique. A strong core assists us in sitting up tall and helps to protect our low backs from risk of injury. According to yoga we are not striving for a "six pack." In fact, yoga advocates for a soft, supple belly that allows room for our organs to function optimally and for our breath to be full and easeful. The optimal expression of a pose, according to yoga texts, includes both steadiness and ease. Core strength contributes to being able to hold a challenging pose with steadiness while also breathing with ease.

If you experience shaking in your muscles while practicing these poses, or any poses, don't resist or try to hide it. In my experience, people carry the belief that shaking is a sign of weakness. One of my teachers calls it "shaking and stirring." When we challenge ourselves we shake and stir things up; that's how we get stronger. Shaking is part of the journey toward steadiness and ease. Having said

> IF YOU EXPERIENCE SHAKING IN YOUR MUSCLES WHILE PRACTICING THESE POSES, OR ANY POSES, DON'T RESIST OR TRY TO HIDE IT.

that, it's also important to listen to your body and not push so hard that you're reinforcing imbalances in your body. The following are my favorite core strengtheners for paddlers.

*Opposite: Handstand at Folly
Beach, South Carolina.*

TABLE TOP POSE

Table top pose is a gentle core strengthener.

> Come to hands and knees on the mat, placing your hands mindfully underneath your shoulders. Spread your fingers. Press the fingertip pads and the balls of the index fingers into the mat, taking the weight out of the heels of your hands.

> Bring your left knee to the center line of the mat, and inhale your right leg up and back, lifting from the inner thigh of the right leg.

> Take the sitz bones back and apart as you continue to lift the inner thigh of the right leg.

> Take your front low ribs down, expand the back ribs, and lengthen through the upper spine and out the crown of the head. Notice how this action engages the core.

> Hold for five deep and easy breaths.

> If you want more challenge, extend your left arm forward.

> Hold for five deep and easy breaths.

> Come back to all fours. Pause and notice the sensations in your body and mind.

> Switch sides and repeat.

PLANK ON KNEES

> Come to hands and knees on the mat, placing your hands mindfully underneath your shoulders. Spread your fingers. Press the fingertip pads and the balls of the index fingers into the mat, taking the weight out of the heels of your hands.

> Walk your knees back a few inches until you feel your core engage.

> Draw the sitz bones back and apart.

> Take your front low ribs down, expand the back ribs, and lengthen through the upper spine and out the crown of the head. Notice how this action engages the core.

> Hold for five deep and easy breaths.

> If your body starts shaking, then let it shake!

FULL PLANK

> Come to hands and knees on the mat, placing your hands mindfully underneath your shoulders. Spread your fingers. Press the fingertip pads and the balls of the index fingers into the mat, taking the weight out of the heels of your hands.

> Walk your feet back to lift your knees off the floor.

> Draw the sitz bones back and apart, and press your hands into the floor to fill up the back ribs.

> Take your front low ribs down, expand the back ribs, and lengthen through the upper spine and out the crown of the head. Notice how this action engages the core.

> Extend back from the hips out the soles of the feet and from the hips forward out the crown of the head.

> Hold for five deep and easy breaths.

TWISTS

THE OBLIQUES ARE KEY MUSCLES in the movement of torso rotation and tend to be chronically contracted in paddlers. Twists help to stretch the obliques, give our internal organs a good massage, stimulate digestion, and calm the nervous system. Below are my favorite twists for paddlers.

Opposite: Spring colors on
Biltmore Lake, Asheville,
North Carolina.
Left photo by Spencer Cooke

SIMPLE SEATED TWIST

This is a gentle twist that invites the obliques to lengthen, keeps your spine supple, gives a gentle massage to internal organs, and stimulates your digestive fire.

> Take a comfortable cross-legged seat on your mat. Sit up on a few blankets if it helps you to sit comfortably for several minutes.

> Reach back and move the flesh out from underneath your sitz bones to sit up taller.

> Exhale. Take your left hand to your right knee and your right hand behind you, twisting to the right.

> Take the sitz bones back and apart.

> Inhale to take your front low ribs down, expand the back ribs, and lengthen through the upper spine and out the crown of the head.

> Exhale to twist a little deeper. Hold for five deep and easy breaths.

> Inhale to come forward and release the pose.

> Pause and notice the sensations in your body and your mind.

> Switch sides and repeat.

FISH HALF-TWIST

This is a deeper twist that lengthens the obliques, gives the internal organs a squeeze, cultivates suppleness in the spine, offers a gentle opening in the chest and shoulders, and gives a gentle stretch to the glute of the bent leg.

> Take a seat on your mat.

> Extend your left leg forward on the mat.

> Bend your right knee, and place the right foot flat on the mat on the outside of the left leg.

> Reach back and move the flesh out from underneath your sitz bones to sit up taller.

> Inhale to extend out the crown of the head.

> Exhale, twist your navel toward the right, hug your right knee with your left arm, and place your right hand behind you for support. Press the hand into the mat and take the right shoulder blade back and down.

> Inhale to take your front low ribs down, expand the back ribs, and lengthen through the upper spine and out the crown of the head.

> Exhale to twist a little deeper.

> Hold for five deep and easy breaths.

> To go deeper in the twist, you can take your left elbow to the outside of your right knee. This will invite a deeper twist.

RECLINED TWIST

This is a lovely, relaxing twist that feels wonderful right before relaxation pose. It's a passive stretch of the obliques that brings suppleness to the spine, stimulates your digestive fire, and is soothing to your nervous system. When the arms are extended out from the shoulders, it offers a chest opener and shoulder stretch.

> Lie on your back with your knees bent and feet flat on the mat.

> Press into your feet to lift your hips slightly off the floor, then shift them over to the left a few inches and set them down.

> Bend your knees at a 90-degree angle so that your thighs are perpendicular to your body and your shins are parallel to the floor.

> Inhale here, and on your exhale bring your knees to the right and all the way to the floor.

> If it's available to you, keep your knees bent at the 90-degree angle to get the deepest possible twist.

> Extend the arms out from the shoulders and soften the left shoulder blade toward the floor.

> Hold for five deep and easy breaths.

> Inhale the knees back to center, place the feet on the floor, and shift the hips back to center.

> Pause and notice the sensations in your body and your mind.

> Switch sides and repeat.

RELAXATION

CHAPTER 4 OUTLINES THE BENEFITS of relaxation and stress management in relation to the breath. One breath cycle is both a receiving (inhale) and a giving (exhale). Our bodies are wired to receive and to give at a cellular level. Each cell takes in nutrition and eliminates waste. We take in fuel and output energy. Our culture is focused almost exclusively on expending energy. Keep moving, keep busy, and keep striving. We fuel our bodies on the move and sacrifice sleep in the name of ambition. Slowing down and rejuvenating are generally perceived as signs of weakness and failure. What do you most often hear when you ask someone how they're doing? The answer is usually "busy." If we're busy, our egos feel accomplished.

There's nothing wrong with being up to great things in life. It's important to share our unique gifts with the world, and that requires action and energy. Having said that, it is unrealistic to think that our bodies and minds can thrive while expending energy without replenishment. Top athletes know that recovery days are important to enhance performance. Our muscles perform optimally when they can contract fully *and* yield fully, and we perform better in life when we know how to take action *and* relax. The main message of this book focuses on moving toward balance by counteracting imbalances. Sometimes that counteraction is about letting go and *not* doing.

The benefits of relaxation and stress management are many (see chapter 4). Relaxation is just as important a pose for paddlers as any other pose in this book. Take the time to include it at the end of every practice and whenever you need a rest.

Opposite: Floating relaxation pose on Lake Julian, Asheville, North Carolina.

RELAXATION POSE

> Lie on your back with your legs extended, arms by your sides and palms facing up. Your arms should feel at ease—not too close to your body and not too far away.

> Allow your legs to relax and externally rotate.

> Take three deep breaths, inhaling through the nose and exhaling out the mouth to release any tension.

> Let go of controlling the breath, and simply observe the path of the breath through the body.

> Notice the thoughts in your mind, acknowledge them, and let them float away as if they were clouds passing by overhead, or a leaf floating away downstream in the current. Return your attention to the path of your breath through your body.

> Hold for a minimum of five minutes at the end of your practice, or perform this pose independent of your practice to encourage deep relaxation.

> To come out of the pose, hug your knees into your chest, roll over onto your right side, and pause there until you're ready to press yourself up to a seated position.

> Notice the sensations in your body and mind.

RELAXATION POSE WITH KNEE SUPPORT

> If you feel tension in your low back when you lie in relaxation pose, then roll up a blanket or get a bolster and place it under your knees for support. You may need to use multiple blankets or bolsters. Make yourself comfortable so that you can relax completely.

RELAXATION POSE WITH CHEST OPENER

To allow the chest to open in relaxation pose, lie over a bolster.

> Place the bolster lengthwise on the mat.

> Sit with the bolster against your low back.

> Lie back on the bolster and allow your arms to rest out from your body, palms up.

> Another option is to lie on a bolster and have support under your knees.

> Come into relaxation pose and place the sandbags on your thighs so that the weight is evenly distributed and they won't fall off.

> Allow your thighs to release under the weight.

> Grasp the outer edges of your mat with your hands, and take the sitz bones back and apart.

> Lift your back off the mat and pull down with your hands to lengthen your torso out of your lower body.

RELAXATION POSE WITH WEIGHT ON THE THIGHS

In my experience, placing sandbags on the thighs during relaxation helps to relieve low back discomfort by releasing the hip flexors and the quads. It is also deeply relaxing and restful.

> Take your front low ribs down, expand the back ribs, and lengthen out the crown of the head.

> Take your back to the floor, pressing the back ribs into the mat.

> Take three deep breaths, inhaling through the nose and exhaling out the mouth to release any tension.

> Let go of controlling the breath, and simply observe the path of the breath through the body.

> Notice the thoughts in your mind, acknowledge them, and let them float away as if they were clouds passing by overhead, or a leaf floating downstream in the current. Return your attention to the path of the breath through the body.

> Hold for a minimum of five minutes.

> To come out of the pose, gently remove the sandbags, extend your arms overhead for a full-body stretch, hug your knees to your chest, roll over onto your right side, and push yourself up to sitting.

LEGS UP THE WALL

Legs up the wall is one of the most relaxing yoga poses and feels wonderful after hours of traveling. I highly recommend practicing this pose to wind down before bed, or anytime you want to unwind.

> Place your yoga mat with a short edge (front or back) against a wall.

> Sit on the mat right next to the wall with one hip touching the wall.

> Turn toward the wall and lie back with your legs up the wall.

> You may have to shift forward until your butt is against the wall.

> Let your arms relax by your sides, palms facing up, not too close and not too far away from the body.

> Let go of controlling the breath, and simply observe the path of the breath through the body.

> Notice the thoughts in your mind, acknowledge them, and let them float away as if they were clouds passing by overhead, or a leaf floating downstream in the current. Return your attention to the path of the breath through the body.

> Hold for as long as feels good, and enjoy the benefits of relaxation and rejuvenation.

SEQUENCING AND HOME PRACTICE

DEVELOPING A HOME PRACTICE can enhance the benefits of your yoga practice in many ways. A consistent practice on most days, even if it is only ten minutes, offers more benefits than attending an hour-and-a-half class once a month. According to Ayurveda (the 5,000-year-old system of health and the sister science to yoga), the choices we make and the habits we keep on a daily basis are what contribute to the state of our health. For that reason Ayurveda puts a lot of focus on developing a daily routine that supports well-being. Yoga is an important part of that routine for the benefits we've discussed so far in this book. They include self-awareness, stress management, focus, strength, balance, and flexibility.

The following sequences are examples of how you can put routines together. For this book I chose three sequencing levels: gentle, active, and vigorous. You can combine vigorous poses with gentle poses too. There are a few common sequencing strategies. One is to start gentle, build up to vigorous, and then transition back to gentle. Another would be to start active, build up to vigorous, and finish with gentle.

Additionally, think about balancing the effects of one pose with another. A common example is balancing a back bend with a forward fold. Back bends are stimulating, while forward folds are calming. Twists are calming to the nervous system, and are therefore nice to do as prep for relaxation pose. Remember that our muscles want to move through their full range of motion. If you're paying attention to your body, it will usually guide you to what is needed for balance. Make the time, and find the joy in exploring poses and movements that help to balance your body and mind.

CREATING A YOGA ROUTINE

Anyone can create their own yoga routine. The hardest part is pulling out your mat and stepping onto it. If you can manage that, then you're well on your way. Here are some general tips for creating and exploring yoga sequencing at home:

- Create a space that supports your yoga practice. Make it clutter-free, with decor that inspires you. In an ideal world it would be a room that is only used for yoga, meditation, and breathwork. But it's important to work with what you've got. It doesn't have to be a big space or a whole room.

- Get on your mat and start moving. It doesn't matter what position you start in. It could be standing, on all fours, lying on your back, or sitting. There is no right or wrong. Get into a shape, find your breath, and pause to tune into your body. Your body will tell you what to do next if you're paying attention. Continue to pay attention, and move from posture to posture, letting your body's natural intelligence lead the way. Don't be afraid to make it up as you go along, while keeping a steady connection to your breath.

- If you prefer to have a known and set routine, you can use the short sequences below, adding movements in between to make them flow. Following along with online yoga classes and videos, such as my DVD *Yoga for Kayaking*, can also help. Get to know what works for you, and then commit to doing it with consistency.

- Be creative with movement and breath. Play around with movement in between the poses and when shifting from one pose to another, while moving with your breath. For example, inhale into low lunge, exhale into runner's stretch. You can do this back and forth several times before pausing and holding a pose. This can be beneficial for warming up connective tissue. You can also experiment with moving in and out of a pose. Bridge pose is a good example. Place your arms over your head. Inhale and take them down to the mat by your sides as you lift into bridge pose. Then exhale and take the arms back overhead. Bring your hips back to the floor. Combining movement and breath brings an added flow to your practice, helping to calm and steady the mind and body.

- Play music that inspires your practice. Online streaming services have playlists for yoga and meditation if you don't know where to start.

Gentle Yoga for Paddling Sequence

Lie on your back with your knees bent and feet flat on the mat. Practice five rounds of three-count breathing with your hands resting on your belly.

Windshield wiper pose

Reclining hand to big toe pose

Bridge pose

Reclined twist

Roll up to hands and knees

Child's pose

Cat/Cow

Side plank side stretch variation (both sides)

Down dog

Low lunge

Runner's stretch

Plank

Spider cobra

Low lunge

Runner's stretch

Down dog

Child's pose

Relaxation pose

Active Yoga for Paddling Sequence

Five rounds of three-count belly breathing in mountain pose with hands in prayer position in front of the heart

Six Sun salutations as warm-up

Palm tree

Mountain pose with hands behind back

Standing forward fold with hands behind back

High lunge

Low lunge holding back foot

Plank

Shoulder blade push-ups

Cobra

Down dog

High lunge

Low lunge holding back foot

Down dog

Plank

Thigh stretch on belly both sides

Child's pose

Windshield wiper pose

Bridge pose

Reclining hand to big toe pose

Reclined twist

Relaxation pose

Vigorous Yoga for Paddling Sequence

Five rounds of three-count belly breathing in mountain pose with hands in prayer position in front of the heart

Twelve sun salutations

Palm tree

Mountain pose with hands behind back

Standing forward fold

High lunge

Warrior II

Side angle stretch

Triangle pose

Half moon

Plank

Side plank

Plank

Side plank

Shoulder blade push-ups

Cobra/Up dog

Down dog

High lunge

Warrior II

Side angle stretch

Triangle pose

Half moon

Standing forward fold

Squat to sitting

Fish half-twist

Wheel

Windshield wiper pose

Reclining hand to big toe pose

Reclined twist

Relaxation pose

SUP YOGA BASICS

SUP YOGA IS AN AWESOME WAY to take your practice outside, connect with nature, and have fun. The extra challenge of balancing on the board builds strength and equilibrium. From an alignment standpoint, SUP yoga can be very informative in making us aware of our imbalances. Muscles that take charge and are overactive on land can go into overdrive when attempting to stabilize us on the board. Our imbalances overcompensate, especially the first few times we're on a SUP. If we're aware of this, we can use SUP yoga as a tool for growing body awareness.

Beyond that, SUP yoga is simply fun, and it can be very relaxing. There is nothing quite like the feeling of floating in relaxation pose under a blue sky with the breeze gently touching your skin and your hands dipped into cool water. It reminds me of being a kid and lying on the ground watching the clouds roll by. How often do we take time to do that as adults?

Speaking directly to yogis, I'm a big advocate of enjoying both the SUP part and the yoga part of SUP yoga. Like any other sport, there are effective and ineffective techniques when it comes to SUPing. A recent study sponsored by the American Council on Exercise found that "novice paddlers did not achieve an adequate heart rate for SUP to be considered moderate-intensity exercise." One of the researchers also pointed out, "The more proficient you are on the water—or in any type of workout, for that matter—the better workout you will get." I bring this up not because I think everyone who SUPs should want a workout, but to highlight the fact that learning to paddle effectively can have a positive impact on your SUP experience. The same is true of SUP

Opposite: Yoga on water in Asheville, North Carolina.

Paddling with a furry friend makes for a lot of fun on the water!

yoga. There is more to SUP than meets the eye. I recommend seeking out instruction from a competent and certified SUP instructor. The American Canoe Association is a good resource for quality instruction and certifications.

From a water safety standpoint, there is also a lot to think about. Wind, water, waves, and weather are all factors that we can't control and that we don't have to think about in a yoga studio setting. In a studio we can turn up the heat if it gets too cold or turn on the air-conditioning if it gets too hot. We are protected from the elements when we're inside a yoga room. Out on the water we are exposed to the elements, and they can change quickly. My intention in relaying all this information is to encourage you to take instruction. Learn how to SUP or take a SUP yoga class taught by a competent instructor who is certified in both SUP and yoga.

That way you can learn to paddle and set yourself up to have the safest, most positive SUP yoga experience.

You will need a few basic pieces of equipment to practice SUP yoga: a board, a paddle, a leash, a personal flotation device (PFD), and an anchor. Most SUP yoga classes provide all the gear if you don't have it. The type of board you use for SUP yoga matters. Boards designed for fitness and yoga tend to be more stable and have deck padding that covers the entire board for more practice surface area. They also have multiple attachment points for anchors (you can attach at the nose or the tail) and have attachments through which you can run bungee cords to secure your water bottle and other gear. The best boards for yoga are both fun to paddle and stable enough for a yoga practice.

Your leash serves a few purposes. It's an important piece of safety gear that attaches you to your board while you paddle out to your anchor system or spot. Once you're anchored, your leash can secure your paddle while it floats in the water.

A PFD is a very important piece of safety equipment. Coast Guard–approved inflatable PFDs that look like fanny packs make wearing one easy and practical. As an American Canoe Association SUP Yoga Endorser, I follow their policy of wearing my inflatable PFD when I teach classes and also require my students to wear them. A PFD doesn't do anyone

All the gear you need for SUP yoga!

who has fallen in the water any good if it's left on the board. Inflatable PFDs are small and easy to move around so that they are out of the way while you practice. You'll notice that mine changes position on my body in the photos depending on what pose I'm practicing. I've even had

A simple brick anchor tied off to the attachemnt point at the nose with a cam strap or rope makes anchoring easy.

some students choose to wear regular, inherently buoyant PFDs during SUP yoga because it made them feel more comfortable about falling into the water.

An anchor is used in SUP yoga to keep the board from floating away in yoga bliss. This is especially important if you're practicing on a body of water with boat traffic, other paddling traffic, any amount of current, or an area with a lot of wind. Some SUP yoga teachers have developed highly effective anchor systems that multiple boards can clip into. There are even floating docks designed specifically for SUP yoga. My anchor of choice for individual board anchoring is a plain ol' brick or a mushroom anchor with about 15 feet of rope or a cam strap attached to it. It really doesn't have to be complicated, but it does have to be heavy enough to counteract your weight and any wind/current. The rope attaching the anchor to the board also has to be long enough so that the anchor can reach the bottom. I tie the rope to the leash loop and voila! You can take up any slack in the rope and tie it off so that the board travels even less. If you're floating around on a calm, flat, protected body of water with no motorized boat traffic, then you may choose to not use an anchor.

Considerations for SUP Yoga

It's tempting to get on a board and try the most challenging poses that you can do on land. As I mentioned earlier, the extra challenge of balancing on a SUP can put muscle imbalances into overdrive. Ignoring this element of SUP yoga can lead to an increased risk of injury. This is especially true when yogis jump on a board and immediately try to do inversions.

I don't cover inversions in this book because I feel they are best cultivated in the physical presence of a competent instructor. The neck and spine are both key to structural integrity. Protecting them by working progressively and mindfully with inversions on land is advisable. Getting injured because of trying to do a headstand on a board (or on land) without prep just seems silly and preventable.

I recommend keeping your exploration of SUP yoga simple. Start seated or on all fours, and move around on this plane. As you gain balance and confidence, you can start moving into poses with two or three points of contact on the board, such as bridge pose or low lunge.

You can practice most of the poses included in earlier chapters on a SUP once you've had some experience with them on land. I've chosen a few poses to focus on in this chapter to give you an idea of techniques that can be helpful in providing more stability. To eliminate repetition, I won't take you through the following poses step-by-step; you can refer back to previous chapters for that. Instead I'll focus on small adjustments that you can make in the poses to enhance balance and stability while practicing on the board. I'll also introduce variation progressions for certain poses that move from most stable to most challenging.

Transitions between poses can feel more challenging at first than the poses themselves. Move slowly and from the core for maximum stability. Play around with the alignment principles outlined in chapter 3, even though they also may feel more challenging on a board.

Small adjustments and modifications can make a big difference in SUP yoga. One of the benefits of practicing yoga on a SUP is that it helps you to become aware

> " ONE OF THE BENEFITS OF PRACTICING YOGA ON A SUP IS THAT IT HELPS YOU TO BECOME AWARE OF THE SUBTLETIES OF YOUR PRACTICE.

of the subtleties of your practice. This is one of the reasons why I don't treat SUP yoga as a fad, but as a valuable tool that can enhance anyone's practice on the mat.

CAT/COW

This is a great pose to start exploring movement on the board while keeping four points of contact (two hands and two knees). For optimal stability, be sure that your navel is over the handle of the board (the center point), your knees are hip width apart, and your hands are placed mindfully under your shoulders. Spread your fingers, and press the fingertip pads and the balls of the index fingers down to take pressure off the wrist.

TABLE TOP BALANCE

You can move from cat/cow to table top to begin exploring balance. A small adjustment for table top on the board is to move the knee that will remain on the board to the centerline (in line with the handle) before you lift and extend the other leg. If you want to explore balance even more, you can lift and extend your opposite arm. The alignment principle that I find most helpful in this pose on the board is taking the front low ribs back, expanding the back ribs, and elongating through the spine. The reason is that moving the ribs back helps to engage the core.

SIDE PLANK VARIATION

In this side plank variation, you can use the rails of the board to help with stabilization. Starting on all fours, take your right foot over the side of the right rail so that your toes are dipped in the water. You can move your back foot toward the left rail for more stability. The wider your stance the more stable you'll feel, while the closer in line the back foot is to the front knee, the less stable you'll feel. You can modify the pose depending on how you are feeling that day and how much you want to challenge yourself.

As you turn open to the sky in this pose, you may feel some unsteadiness. All the alignment principles outlined in chapter 3 will help with steadiness.

DOWN DOG

To feel more stable in down dog on a SUP, I recommend focusing on hand placement and engagement. Spread the fingers wide and press the fingertip pads down into the board while also focusing on pressing the balls of the index fingers down. This takes the weight of the body out of the heels of the hands and distributes it throughout the hands.

On a board every pose becomes a window to where and how we position and balance our bodies. Become aware of how your hands and feet are placed and how that affects your balance on the board. You may also notice that you place more weight into one hand or foot than the other. Notice how this affects your balance and the overall integrity of the pose. In turn, take that knowledge into your practice on the mat. This will enhance your stability and alignment.

LOW LUNGE

Low lunge becomes a more difficult pose to find balance in when practiced on a SUP. It's helpful to start slow. Take a few breaths with your hands on either side of your front foot, engage the alignment principles, and focus on steadying your breath. Once you feel stable in this position, take your hands to your front thigh. For optimal stability, press your front foot strongly into the board, especially your front heel, and also press the back knee down.

If you want more challenge, extend your arms overhead while looking to the horizon in front of you. Once you feel good with that, lift your gaze to the sky. You may even curl back, while also holding an awareness of the alignment principles. Lifting the gaze makes any pose on a SUP more challenging.

HIGH LUNGE

High lunge with the back heel lifted off the board is one of the most difficult standing poses on a SUP besides one-legged balance poses. Start with the heel of the back foot on the board. Play around with this shape and the alignment principles in this shape. Keep a slight bend in the back knee and press both feet into the board strongly. When you're ready, take your back heel off the board. As with low lunge, gaze to the horizon in front of you first, then turn your gaze upward and maybe even curl back. Experiment, and remember to smile, breathe, and relax!

If you feel that you want a more stable base on the board in this pose, take a wider stance. For example, if your right foot is forward and your left foot is back, take your right foot a few inches to the right and your left foot a few inches to the left.

WARRIOR II

In my practice, I view warrior II as the foundation pose for side angle stretch and triangle pose. Having a stable base is key on a board. Taking a wider stance can contribute to more stability. For example, if your right foot is forward and your left foot is back, take your right foot a few inches to the right and your left foot a few inches to the left. When practicing on the board, you sometimes have to let go of certain alignment cues we usually practice on land, such as the front heel being in line with the arch of the back foot. It's OK, there's no right or wrong. This can spark a self-inquiry of how different stances contribute to your practice.

Another key action is pressing the outside edge of the back foot strongly into the board. You can get away with having the back foot partially lifted on the mat and still feel stable, but when the outer edge of the back foot is lifted off the board, it reduces the surface area of connection to the board. The more surface area that is on the board, the more stability you have. Other benefits of engaging the outer edge of the back foot in this pose—and any pose with this foot positioning—include strengthening and engagement of the inner thigh of the back leg as well as distribution of weight through both feet. These benefits add strength and stability to the pose on a SUP and on land.

> **HAVING A STABLE BASE IS KEY ON A BOARD. TAKING A WIDER STANCE CAN CONTRIBUTE TO MORE STABILITY.**

Pressing the front heel into the board strongly is important in this pose for activating the back of the front leg, which increases stability. Remember that your heels are designed to bear weight. Let them do their job, and you'll build strength and stability.

The last thing I'd like to address for the warrior poses and triangle pose is an awareness of core engagement and how to hold the upper body. I see more people fall off their boards practicing these poses than during any other poses (besides balance poses on one foot or arm balances). What I've seen is practitioners leaning their upper bodies back into the poses, especially side angle and triangle, which can result in falling off the board. Again, this is something we can get away with on the mat, because the floor doesn't shift underneath us, and we can shift more weight into the bottom hand on the floor for stability. The instability of a SUP feels different.

To increase stability when practicing on a SUP, I recommend keeping a bend in the back knee in warrior, and in both knees in triangle, to engage the backs of the legs. Move slowly, and use the alignment principles from chapter 3. They will help to engage the core so that the trunk retains integrity and doesn't fall back. Falling or leaning back, even an inch or two, on a SUP in these poses usually equates to falling off the board. That's not a big deal. Falling off the board can be refreshing and fun. Falling means that we are challenging ourselves and practicing courage. Anytime we take risks in life, there is a chance of falling on our faces. Falling provides us with learning opportunities that help us to grow.

WIDE LEGGED FORWARD FOLD

When taking a wide stance toward the side of a SUP, the weighting of the heels is key for balance and stability. Plant your feet on the midline of the board or a little farther back for a forward fold. Engage the alignment principles, especially taking the sitz bones back and apart, keeping a slight bend in both knees and weighting the heels.

RELAXATION POSE

This is the best part of SUP yoga! I've already mentioned it above, but relaxation pose on a SUP is very peaceful. Imagine that any stress, anxiety, or worry is flowing from your body, out your fingertips and into the water. Let the water absorb it and carry it away, and give gratitude for the water's ability to cleanse.

Every day I give gratitude for the water on our planet. Water is key in sustaining life, yet unfortunately, it has been, and is being, greatly mistreated and contaminated. According to www.water.org, one in ten people on the planet lacks access to safe water. It's up to us to take care of our water through awareness, lifestyle, and choices. As paddlers who spend a lot of time on the water and have direct experiences with water quality, we can have a big impact. One of the aspects of teaching SUP yoga, SUP, and kayaking that I enjoy the most is introducing people to, and growing their awareness of, the importance of water and water quality. Relaxation pose on a SUP provides deep relaxation and a space for you to connect with this important element.

NOTES

1   Erich Schiffmann, *Yoga The Spirit and Practice of Moving Into Stillness*, Pocket Books Non-Fiction, pp. 29–30.

2   Study, "Relaxation Response and Resiliency Training and Its Effect on Healthcare Resource Utilization," by James E. Stahl, Michelle L. Dossett, A. Scott LaJoie, John W. Denninger, Darshan H. Mehta, Roberta Goldman, Gregory L. Fricchione, and Herbert Benson. Published October 13, 2015.

3   Article, "Harvard Scientist Finds Benefits of Meditation," by Makiku Kitamura. November 24, 2013, bloomberg.com.

4   Article, "Sweat the Small Stuff," by Peter King. August 12, 2014, mmqb.si.com.

5   Article, "Beyond Downward Dog: The Rise of Yoga in the NBA and other Pro Sports," by Sarah Toland. June 27, 2014, si.com.

6   Article, "Harvard Scientist Finds Benefits of Meditation," by Makiku Kitamura. November 24, 2013, bloomberg.com.

7   *Yoga Anatomy,* by Leslie Kaminoff, 2007, Human Kinetics.

INDEX

ABOUT THE AUTHOR

Anna Levesque is a leading expert on kayak instruction for women and yoga for paddling. Named one of the most inspirational paddlers alive by *Canoe & Kayak* magazine, Anna's twenty-plus years of experience as an accomplished international competitor and instructor has landed her in mainstream publications such as *Time*, *Shape*, and *Self* magazines.

She is the founder/director of www.water-girlsatplay.com and www.mindbodypaddle .com, and has taught thousands of paddlers worldwide. Anna has produced four instructional kayaking DVDs for women, a *Yoga for*

Kayaking DVD, and short downloadable yoga for kayaking segments on Vimeo that have sold over 6,500 copies combined.

Anna is an American Canoe Association Whitewater Kayak and Stand-Up Paddleboard Instructor Trainer, and a SUP Yoga Endorser. She is also a certified Ayurveda Health Counselor and a 500 RYT with Yoga Alliance who coaches and supports clients in cultivating vitality, self-care, and healthy digestion through effective diet and lifestyle choices.

She is a brand ambassador for Dagger Kayaks, BIC SUP, Werner Paddles, Kokatat Watersports Wear, and Shred Ready Helmets.

She lives in Asheville, North Carolina, with her husband, Andrew, and their schnoodle, Ceiba.

Instagram: annaclevesque
Facebook: www.facebook.com/anna.levesque2
www.mindbodypaddle.com
www.watergirlsatplay.com

For more about photographer **Scott Martin**, visit his website: www.scottmartin images.com.